Quantum Healing
Through
Radical Forgiveness

By COLIN C.TIPPING

A QEMS Resource Book

Quantum Healing Through Radical Forgiveness

Published in August, 2004

Abridged from Radical Forgiveness: Making Room for the Miracle
Original Version Published in October, 1997
Second Edition: Published in Spring, 2002

Radical Forgiveness is a trademark of Global 13 Publications and the Institute of Radical Forgiveness Therapy and Coaching, Inc.

ISBN 0-9704814-5-4

Global 13 Publications, Inc.
26 Briar Gate Lane,
Marietta GA 30066
sales@radicalforgiveness.com

Website: www.radicalforgiveness.com
Cover Design: Deborah Hill
Illustrations: JoAnna Tipping

Contents

Foreword: *"Read-Me"*

Computer software frequently comes with a "read me" section. This is usually a written addendum or an update, telling you something important about the program itself that is not already included. It might even be a warning.

This book is a condensed version of my original book, *Radical Forgiveness: Making Room for the Miracle,* first published in 1997. As such, it does need a "read-me" foreword that carries a warning.

The warning is, *don't believe a word of it!* And don't give up any of your existing beliefs, especially your religious ones. That's because Radical Forgiveness is not in itself a belief system and doesn't require one. It is no threat in this regard.

Beliefs reside in the intellect and Radical Forgiveness is a process that completely bypasses the intellect. It relies, not on your intellectual intelligence, but on your spiritual intelligence, a concept I explain in depth in the other book in this kit, *Spiritual Intelligence at Work.* Spiritual Intelligence is a basic facility we all have that connects us to the unseen world of spirit and is totally independent of any beliefs we have about that world.

Even though I try to argue my case persuasively throughout this book and in *Spiritual Intelligence At Work*, I base it all, not on fixed beliefs, but on a set of assumptions I make about the spiritual world. These are set out briefly in Chapter Two. I have no way of knowing whether these assumptions are true or false, and frankly, I don't care.

I don't care because it is enough for me to observe what happens when people just become willing to try the process based on those assumptions — Radical Forgiveness. The results are often quite staggering. People's lives change dramatically. Problems simply dissolve. Situations get resolved, seemingly on their own. For me it is proof enough. I don't need a belief system. And you don't have to change yours. In fact, the only reason I refer to those assumptions is that I need some way to arrange the material cognitively so we can have a reasonable conversation about what is, in the end, still unknowable, unexplainable and totally mysterious.

Additionally, I have discovered that the only requirement for success with Radical Forgiveness is to have just the tiniest amount of willingness to be open to one basic assumption. This says that, no matter how unlikely or how absurd the idea seems, everything is divinely guided and happens for a reason that is usually beyond our capacity to comprehend. Also, that there are no accidents and we are being served in some way by everything that occurs in our life. In other words, that the hand of God is in every aspect of our life and God does not make mistakes. Life provides us with exactly the right situations from which to

2

grow and learn. And we actually have a hand in creating those opportunities, thanks to our own spiritual intelligence. Just being momentarily open to that idea as a possibility — a remote possibility even — is not accepting it as a belief. Neither is it throwing away beliefs that you already have that might seem to contradict this radical idea. In fact, the more skeptical you are, the better I like it. All I ask is that you try it.

Let me make it clear that this book is not an essential part of the QEMS kit. I have included it simply as additional resource material for those who would like to understand the thinking that led to me to want to bring the Radical Forgiveness experience to the corporate world in the form of QEMS.

I also include it for those who not only see the value in using this technology to prevent conflict at work, but who also recognize it as a way to improve their own lives, increase their happiness and unlock their potential to be all they can be as human beings.

It will speak, as the other version has, to those who have done their best to deal with their own internal pain caused by abuse, betrayal, abandonment and so on, and have failed largely for the want of a good technology to help them deal with it. Everywhere we look — in the newspapers, TV, and even in our own personal lives, we see examples of egregiously hurt victims. We read, for example, that at least one out of every five adults in America today was either physically or sexually abused as a child.

3

Traditional forgiveness has failed them, psychological therapy has not given them the relief they hoped for, and the self-help books have offered little more than affirmations and "think positive — feel-good" material. Whereas these do little to help heal deep wounds, Radical Forgiveness definitely has the potential to do so. It is fast, easy to do, simple and therapy-free.

It will speak also to those who have medicated their pain with food, alcohol, drugs, sex and other addictions that caused them to pack on the weight, create sickness in their bodies and ruin their lives. Radical Forgiveness helps to heal the pain that underlie those addictive behaviors.

The Radical Forgiveness technology is the quickest and simplest way to rid oneself of that toxicity because it uses, not psychological processes which rely on the intellectual and emotional intelligence of the person, both of which vary widely from person to person, but on spiritual intelligence which we all share equally. It is a technology whose time has come.

I do recognize that the assumptions I am presenting here might be extremely challenging for someone severely victimized and still carrying a lot of pain. I ask only that you read this book with an open mind and see whether or not you feel better after reading it. If you notice even a slight improvement, try one of the tools and then see if it makes a difference in your life. I trust that it will.

Colin Tipping   Atlanta, 2004

PART ONE
A Radical Healing

Author's Note

*T*o give you, the reader, an understanding of what I call Radical Forgiveness, I have presented the following true account of how this process saved my sister's marriage and changed her life. Since that time, Radical Forgiveness has positively impacted the lives of countless others, for not long after this episode with my sister, I realized that the process could be used as a form of help quite different from traditional psychotherapy and relationship counseling. I now offer what I call Radical Forgiveness Coaching to clients in my private practice and in my workshops, and seldom need to do the kind of therapy I once did. This is because I find that problems more or less disappear when you teach people how to use the tools of Radical Forgiveness.

C.T.

1: Jill's Story

As soon as I saw my sister Jill emerge into the lobby of Atlanta's Hartsfield International Airport, I knew something was wrong. She had never hidden her feelings well, and it was apparent to me that she was in emotional pain.

Jill had flown from England to the United States with my brother John, whom I had not seen for sixteen years. He had emigrated from England to Australia in 1972 and I to America in 1984 — thus Jill was, and still is, the only one of the three siblings living in England. John had made a trip home, and this trip to Atlanta represented the last leg of his return journey. Jill accompanied him to Atlanta so she could visit me and my wife JoAnna for a couple of weeks and see him off to Australia from there.

After the initial hugging and kissing and a certain amount of awkwardness, we set out for the hotel. I had arranged rooms for one night so JoAnna and I could show them Atlanta the next day before driving north to our home.

As soon as the first opportunity for serious discussion presented itself, Jill said, "Colin, things are not good at home. Jeff and I might be splitting up."

7

Despite the fact that I had noticed that something seemed wrong with my sister, this announcement surprised me. I had always thought she and her husband Jeff were happy in their six-year marriage. Both had been married before, but this relationship had seemed strong. Jeff had three kids with his previous wife, while Jill had four. Her youngest son, Paul, was the only one still living at home.

"What's going on?" I asked.

"Well, it's all quite bizarre, and I don't quite know where to begin," she replied. "Jeff is acting really strange, and I can't stand much more of it. We've gotten to the point where we can't talk to each other anymore. It's killing me. He has totally turned away from me and says that it's all my fault."

"Tell me about it," I said, glancing at John, who responded by rolling his eyes. He'd stayed at their house for a week prior to flying to Atlanta, and I guessed by his demeanor that he'd heard enough of this subject to last him a while.

"Do you remember Jeff's eldest daughter Lorraine?" Jill asked. I nodded. "Well, her husband got killed in a car crash about a year ago. Ever since then, she and Jeff have developed this really weird relationship. Any time she calls, he fawns over her, calling her 'Love,' and spending hours talking to her in hushed tones. You'd think they were lovers, not father and daughter. If he's in the middle of something and she calls, he drops everything to talk with her. If she comes to our home, he acts just the same — if not

8

worse. They huddle together in this deep and hushed conversation that excludes everyone else, especially me. I can hardly stand it. I feel she has become the center of his life, and I hardly figure in at all. I feel totally shut out and ignored."

She went on and on, offering more details of the strange family dynamic that had developed. JoAnna and I listened attentively. We wondered aloud about the cause of Jeff's behavior and were generally sympathetic. We made suggestions as to how she might talk to him about his behavior and generally struggled to find a way to fix things, as would any concerned brother and sister-in-law. John was supportive and offered his perspective on the situation as well.

What seemed strange and suspicious to me was the uncharacteristic nature of Jeff's behavior. The Jeff I knew was affectionate with his daughters and certainly co-dependent enough to badly need their approval and love, but I had never seen him behave in the manner Jill described. I had always known him as caring and affectionate towards Jill. In fact, I found it hard to believe that he would treat her quite so cruelly. I found it easy to understand why this situation made Jill unhappy and how Jeff's insistence that she was imagining it all and making herself mentally ill over it, made it all so much worse for her.

The conversation continued all the next day. I began to get a picture of what might be going on between Jill and Jeff from a Radical Forgiveness standpoint but decided not to mention it — at least not right away. She was too caught up in the drama of the situation and wouldn't have been able to hear and understand what I had to say. Radical Forgiveness is based on a very broad spiritual perspective that was not our shared reality when we were all still living in England. Feeling certain that both she and John were unaware of my beliefs underlying Radical Forgiveness, I felt the time had not yet arrived to introduce so challenging a thought as *this is perfect just the way it is: and an opportunity to heal.*

However, after the second day of verbally going round and round about the problem, I decided the time was near for me to try the Radical Forgiveness approach. This would require that my sister open up to the possibility that something beyond the obvious was happening — something that was purposeful, divinely guided, and intended for her highest good. Yet she was so committed to being the *victim* in the situation, I wasn't sure I could get her to hear an interpretation of Jeff's behavior that would take her out of that role.

However, just as my sister began yet another repetition of what she had said the day before, I decided to intervene. Tentatively, I said, "Jill, are you willing to look at this situation differently? Would you be open to me giving you a quite different interpretation of what is happening?"

She looked at me quizzically, as if she were wondering, *'How can there possibly be another interpretation? It is how it is!'* However, I have a certain track record with Jill in that I had helped her solve a relationship problem before, so she trusted me enough to say, "Well, I guess so. What do you have in mind?"

This was the opening I was waiting for. "What I'm going to say may sound strange, but try not to question it until I have finished. Just stay open to the possibility that what I am saying is true, and see whether or not what I say makes sense to you in any way at all."

Until this time, John had done his best to stay attentive to Jill, but the constant repetitive conversation about Jeff had begun to bore him tremendously. In fact, he had largely tuned her out. However, I was acutely aware that my interjection caused John to perk up and begin listening again.

"What you have described to us, Jill, certainly represents the truth as you see it," I began. "I have not the slightest doubt in my mind that this is occurring just as you say it is. Besides, John has witnessed much of the situation over the last three weeks and confirms your story, right, John?" I queried, turning toward my brother.

"Absolutely," he confirmed. "I saw it going on a lot, just as Jill says. I thought it was pretty strange and, quite honestly, much of the time I felt awkward being there."

"I'm not surprised," I said. "Anyway Jill, I want you to know that nothing I am going to say negates what you have said or invalidates your story. I believe that it happened the way you said it happened. Let me, however, give you a hint of what might be going on underneath this situation."

11

"What do you mean, *underneath the situation,*" Jill asked, eyeing me suspiciously.

"It's perfectly natural to think that everything *out there* is *all* there is to reality," I explained. "But maybe there's a whole lot more happening beneath that reality. We don't perceive anything else going on because our five senses are inadequate to the task. But that doesn't mean it isn't occurring.

"Take your situation. You and Jeff have this drama going on. That much is clear. What if, beneath the drama, something of a more spiritual nature was happening — same people and same events — but a totally different meaning? What if your two souls were doing the same dance but to a wholly different tune? What if the dance was about you healing? What if you could see this as an opportunity to heal and grow? That would be a very different interpretation, would it not?"

Both she and John looked at me as if I were now speaking a foreign language. I decided to back off from the explanation and to go directly for the experience.

"Looking back over the last three months or so, Jill," I went on. "What did you feel mostly when you saw Jeff behaving so lovingly towards his daughter Lorraine?"

"Anger mostly," she said, but continued thinking about it. "Frustration," she added. Then, after a long pause, "and sadness. I really feel sad." Tears welled up in her eyes. "I feel so alone and unloved," she said and began sobbing quietly. "It wouldn't be so bad if I thought he couldn't show love, but he can and he does — but with *her!"*

She spat the last few words out with vehemence and rage and began to sob uncontrollably for the first time since her arrival. She'd shed a few tears prior to this, but she hadn't really let herself cry. Now, at last, she was letting go. I was pleased that Jill had been able to get in touch with her emotions that quickly.

A full ten minutes went by before her crying subsided and I felt she could talk. At that point, I asked, "Jill, can you ever remember feeling this same way when you were a little girl?" Without the slightest hesitation, she said, "Yes." She was not immediately forthcoming about when, so I asked her to explain. It took her a while to respond.

"Dad wouldn't love me either!" she blurted out finally and began to sob again. "I wanted him to love me, but he wouldn't. I thought he couldn't love anyone! Then your daughter came along, Colin. He loved her all right. So why couldn't he love me, Goddamnit?!" She banged her fist hard on the table as she shouted the words and dissolved into more uncontrollable tears.

Jill's reference was to my eldest daughter, Lorraine. Coincidentally, or rather, synchronistically, she and Jeff's eldest daughter have the same name.

Crying felt really good to Jill. Her tears served as a powerful release and possibly a turning point for her. A real breakthrough might not be far away, I thought. I needed to keep nudging her forward.

"Tell me about the incident with my daughter Lorraine and Dad," I said.

"Well," Jill said, while composing herself. "I always felt unloved by Dad and really craved his love. He never held my hand or sat me on his lap much. I always felt there must be something wrong with me. When I was older, Mom told me she didn't think Dad was capable of loving anyone, not even her. At that time I had more or less made peace with that. I rationalized that if he wasn't really capable of loving anyone, then it wasn't my fault that he didn't love me. He really didn't love anyone. He hardly ever made a fuss of my kids — his own grandchildren — much less people or kids not his own. He was not a bad father. He just couldn't love. I felt sorry for him."

She cried some more, taking her time now. I knew what she meant about our father. He was a kind and gentle man but very quiet and withdrawn. For the most part, he certainly had seemed emotionally unavailable to anyone.

As Jill became more composed once again, she continued, "I remember a particular day at your house. Your daughter Lorraine was probably about four or five years old. Mom and Dad were visiting from Leicester, and we all came to your house. I saw your Lorraine take Dad's hand. She said, 'Come on, Grandad. Let me show you the garden and all my flowers.' He was like putty in her hands. She led him everywhere and talked and talked and talked, showing him all the flowers. She enchanted him. I watched them out of the window the whole time. When they came back in, he put her on his lap and was as playful and joyful as I had ever seen him.

"I was devastated. *'So, he is able to love after all,'* I thought. If he could love Lorraine, then why not me?" The last few words came out as a whisper followed by deep long tears of grief and sadness, tears held in for all those years.

I figured we had done enough for the time being and suggested we make tea. *(Well, we're English! We always make tea, no matter what!)*

Interpreting Jill's story from a Radical Forgiveness standpoint, I easily saw that Jeff's outwardly strange behavior was unconsciously designed to support Jill in healing her unresolved relationship with her father. If she could see this and recognize the perfection in Jeff's behavior, she could heal her pain, and Jeff's behavior would almost certainly stop. However, I wasn't sure how to explain this to Jill in a way she could understand at this point in time. Luckily, I didn't have to try. She stumbled on the obvious connection by herself.

Later that day she asked me, "Colin, don't you think it's odd that Jeff's daughter and your daughter both have the same name? Come to think of it, both of them are blonde and first-born. Isn't that a strange coincidence! Do you think there's a connection?"

I laughed, and replied, "Absolutely. It's the key to understanding this whole situation."

She looked at me long and hard. "What do you mean?"

"Work it out for yourself," I replied. "What other similarities do you see between that situation with Dad and my Lorraine and your current situation?"

"Well, let's see," said Jill. "Both girls have the same name. Both of them were getting what I don't seem to be able to get from the men in my life."

"What?" I enquired.

"Love," she said in a whisper.

"Go on," I urged gently.

"It seems that your Lorraine was able to get the love from Dad that I couldn't. And Jeff's daughter, Lorraine, gets all the love she wants from her Dad, but at my expense. Oh, my God!" she exclaimed. She really was beginning to understand now.

"But why? I don't understand why. It's a bit frightening! What the heck's going on?" she asked in a panic.

It was time to put the pieces together for her. "Look, Jill," I said. "Let me explain how this works. This happens to be a perfect example of what I was talking about earlier when I said that beneath the drama we call life lies a whole different reality. Believe me, there's nothing to be frightened about. When you see how this works, you will feel more trust, more security, and more peace than you ever thought possible. You'll realize how well we are being supported by the Universe or God, whatever you want to call it, every moment of every day no matter how bad any given situation seems at the time," I said as reassuringly as I could.

"Looked at from a spiritual standpoint, our discomfort in any given situation provides a signal that we are out of alignment with spiritual law and are being given an opportunity to heal something. It may be some original pain or perhaps a toxic belief that stops us from becoming our true selves. We don't often see it from this perspective, however. Rather, we judge the situation and blame others for what is happening, which prevents us from seeing the message or understanding the lesson. This prevents us from healing. If we don't heal whatever needs to be healed, we must create more discomfort until we are literally forced to ask, *'What is going on here?'* Sometimes the message has to become very loud, or the pain extremely intense, before we pay attention. A life-threatening illness, for example, provides a loud message. Yet, even when facing death, some people don't get the connection between what is happening in their lives and the opportunity for healing that it provides.

"In your case, what has come up to be healed this time is your original pain around your father and the fact that he never showed you love. That is what all your current pain

17

and discomfort are about. This particular pain has arisen many times before in different situations, but, because you didn't recognize the opportunity, it never got healed. That's why having yet another opportunity to look at and heal this issue is a gift!"

"A gift?" Jill questioned. "You mean it's a gift because there's a message in it for me? One that I might have gotten a long time ago if I'd been able to see it?"

"Yes," I said. "Had you seen it then, your discomfort would have been less, and you wouldn't be going through this now. No matter. Now is fine too. This is perfect, and you won't now have to produce a life-threatening illness to understand this, like so many people do. You're getting it now; you're beginning to understand and to heal.

"Let me explain to you exactly what happened and how it has affected your life up until now," I said, wanting her to understand clearly the dynamics of her current situation.

"As a little girl, you felt abandoned and unloved by Dad. For a girl, this is devastating. From a developmental standpoint, it is necessary for a young girl to feel loved by her father. Since you didn't feel that love, you concluded that there must something wrong with you. You began to really believe you were unlovable and inherently *not enough*. That belief anchored itself deeply in your subconscious mind and, later, when it came to relationships, began to run your life. In other words, as a way of mirroring your subconscious belief that you were *not enough*, your life always has included actual situations exhibiting to you the fact that you were, indeed, not enough. Life will always prove your beliefs right.

"As a child, the pain of not getting Dad's love was more than you could bear, so you suppressed some of the pain and repressed a whole lot more. When you suppress emotion, you know it's there, but you stuff it down. Repressed emotion, on the other hand, gets buried so deeply in the subconscious mind that you lose awareness of it.

"Later, when you began to realize that your father was not a naturally loving man and probably couldn't love anyone, you began to somewhat rehabilitate or heal yourself from the effects of feeling unloved by him. You probably released some of the suppressed pain and maybe began to give up some part of the belief that you were unlovable. After all, if he couldn't love anyone, maybe it wasn't your fault that he didn't love you.

"Then, along came the bombshell that knocked you right back to square one. When you observed him loving my Lorraine, that triggered your original belief. You said to yourself, *'My father can love after all, but he doesn't love me. It is obviously my fault. I am not enough for my father, and I will never be enough for any man.'* From that point on, you continually created situations in your life to support your belief that you are *not enough.*"

"How have I done that?" Jill interrupted. "I don't see how I have created myself not being enough in my life."

"How was your relationship with Henry, your first husband?" I responded. She had been married to Henry, the father of her four children, for 15 years.

"Not bad in many respects, but he was so unfaithful. He was always looking for opportunities to have sex with other women, and I really hated that."

"Exactly. And you saw him as the villain and you as the victim in that situation. However, the truth is, you attracted him into your life precisely because, at some level, you knew he would prove your belief about not being enough. By being unfaithful, he would support you in being right about yourself."

"Are you trying to say he was doing me a favor? I sure as heck don't buy that!" she said laughingly, but also with some not-too-well-disguised anger.

"Well, he certainly supported your belief, didn't he?" I replied. "You were so *not enough* that he always was on the lookout for other women, for *something more*. If he had done the opposite and consistently treated you as if you were totally enough by being faithful, you would have created some other drama in your life to prove your belief. Your belief about yourself, albeit a totally false one, made it impossible for you to be enough.

"By the same token, had you at that time changed your belief by healing your original pain around your father and changed your belief to *I am enough*, Henry would have immediately stopped propositioning your friends. If he hadn't, you would have felt perfectly happy to leave him and find someone else who would treat you as though you were enough. We always create our reality according to our beliefs. If you want to know what your beliefs are, look at what you have in your life. Life always reflects our beliefs."

Jill seemed a bit perplexed, so I decided to reiterate some of the points I had made. "Each time Henry cheated on you, he gave you the opportunity to heal your original pain around being unloved by Dad. He demonstrated and acted out for you your belief that you were never going to be enough for any man. The first few times this happened, you may have gotten so mad and upset that you could have gotten in touch with the original pain and become acquainted with your belief system about yourself. In fact, his first acts of unfaithfulness represented your first opportunities to practice Radical Forgiveness and to heal your original pain, but you missed them. You made him wrong each time and created yourself as a victim instead, which made healing impossible."

"What do you mean forgiveness?" Jill asked, still looking troubled. "Are you saying I should have forgiven him for seducing my best friend and anyone else he could find who was willing?"

"I am saying that, at that time, he provided you with an opportunity to get in touch with your original pain and to see how a certain belief about yourself was running your

21

life. In so doing, he gave you the opportunity to understand and change your belief, thus healing your original pain. That's what I mean by forgiveness. Can you see why he deserves your forgiveness, Jill?"

"Yes, I think so," she said. "He was reflecting my belief — the one I had formed because I felt so unloved by Dad. He was making me right about not being enough. Is that correct?"

"Yes, and to the extent that he provided you with that opportunity, he deserves credit — actually, more than you realize right now. We have no way of knowing whether he would have stopped his behavior had you healed your issue around Dad at that time — or whether you would have left him. Either way, he would have served you powerfully well. So, in that sense, he deserves not only your forgiveness but your deep gratitude as well. And you know what? It wasn't his fault that you didn't understand the true message behind his behavior.

"I know that it was hard for you to see that he was trying to give you a great gift. That's not how we are taught to think. We're not taught to look at what is going on and to say, 'Look what I have created in my life. Isn't that interesting?' Instead, we are taught to judge, lay blame, accuse, play victim and seek revenge. Neither are we taught to think that our lives are directed by forces other than our own conscious mind — but, in truth, they are.

"In fact, it was Henry's *soul* that tried to help you heal. On the surface, Henry just acted out his sexual addiction, but his soul — working with your soul — chose to use the addiction for your spiritual growth. Recognizing this fact is what Radical Forgiveness is all about. Its purpose lies in seeing the truth behind the apparent circumstances of a situation and recognizing the love that always exists there."

I felt that talking about her current situation would help Jill fully understand the principles I had described. So I said, "Let's take another look at Jeff and see how these principles are operating in your current relationship. In the beginning, Jeff was extremely loving towards you. He really doted on you, did things for you, communicated with you. On the surface, life with Jeff seemed pretty good.

"Remember, though, this didn't fit your picture of yourself — your belief about yourself. According to your belief, you shouldn't have a man who shows you this much love. You are not enough, remember?"

Jill nodded but still looked uncertain and rather perplexed.

"Your soul knows you must heal that belief, so it colludes with Jeff's soul somehow to bring it to your awareness. On the surface it seems that Jeff begins to act strangely and totally out of character. He then taunts you by loving *another* Lorraine, thus acting out with you the very same scenario you had with your father many years ago. He appears to be persecuting you mercilessly, and you feel totally helpless and victimized. Does this describe, more or less, your current situation?" I asked.

"I guess so," Jill said quietly. She wrinkled her brow as she tried to hold on to the new picture of her situation slowly forming in her mind.

"Well, here you are again, Jill, about to make a choice. You must choose whether to heal and to grow — or to be right," I said and smiled.

"If you make the choice people normally make, you will choose to be the victim and make Jeff wrong, which in turn, allows you to be right. After all, his behavior seems quite cruel and unreasonable, and I don't doubt there are many women who wouldn't support you in taking some drastic action in response to it. Haven't most of your friends been saying you should leave him?"

"Yes," she replied. "Everyone says I should get out of the marriage if he doesn't change. I actually thought that you would say that too," she said with a tinge of disappointment.

"A few years ago, I probably would have," I said and laughed. "However, since my introduction to these spiritual principles, my whole way of looking at such situations has changed, as you can see," I said with a wry smile, looking across at John. He grinned but said nothing.

I continued. "So, as you might guess, the other choice might be to recognize that, beneath what seems to be happening on the surface, something else much more meaningful — and potentially very supportive — is going on. The other choice is to accept that Jeff's behavior may possess another message, another meaning, another intent, and that within the situation lies a gift for you."

Jill thought for a while, then said, "Jeff's behavior is so darn bizarre you'd have a hard time coming up with any good reason for it. Maybe something else is going on that I don't yet see. I suppose its similar to what Henry was doing, but it's hard for me to see it with Jeff, because I 'm so confused right now. I can't see beyond what actually is going on."

"That's okay," I said reassuringly. "Look, there's no need to figure it out. Just being willing to entertain the idea that something else is going on is a giant step forward. In fact, the willingness to see the situation differently is the key to your healing. Ninety percent of the healing occurs when you become willing to let in the idea that your soul has lovingly created this situation for you. In becoming willing, you let go of control and surrender it to God. He takes care of the other ten percent. If you can really understand at a deep level and surrender to the idea that God will handle this for you if you turn it over to him, you won't need to do anything at all. The situation and your healing will both get handled automatically.

"However, prior even to this step, you can take a perfectly rational step that enables you to see things differently right away. It involves separating fact from fiction. It means recognizing that your belief has no factual basis whatsoever. It is simply a story you have made up, based on a few facts and a whole lot of interpretation.

25

"We do this all the time. We experience an event and make interpretations about it. Then, we put these two pieces together to create a largely false story about what happened. The story becomes the belief, and we defend it as if it were the truth. It never is, of course.

"In your case, the facts were that Dad didn't hug you, didn't spend time playing with you, didn't hold you, didn't put you on his lap. He did not meet your needs for affection. Those were the facts. On the basis of those facts, you made a crucial assumption: *'Dad doesn't love me.'* Isn't that true?" She nodded.

"However, the fact that he didn't meet your needs doesn't mean that he didn't love you. That's an interpretation. It wasn't true. He was a sexually repressed man and intimacy was scary for him; we know that. Maybe he just didn't know how to express his love in the way you wanted to receive it. Do you remember that super doll house he made you one year for Christmas? I remember him spending countless hours on it in the evenings when you were in bed. Perhaps that was the only way he knew how to express his love for you.

"I'm not making excuses for him or trying to make what you have said, or felt, wrong. I'm just trying to point out how we all make the mistake of thinking that our interpretations represent the truth.

"The next big assumption you made," I continued, "based on the facts *and* your first interpretation that *'Dad doesn't love me,'* was *'It's my fault. There must be something*

26

wrong with me.' That was an even greater lie than the other assumption, don't you agree?" She nodded.

"It isn't surprising that you would come to that conclusion, because that's the way little kids think. Since they perceive that the world revolves around them, they always assume that when things don't go well, it's their fault. When a child first thinks this, the thought is coupled with great pain. To reduce the pain, a child represses it, but this action actually makes it all the harder to get rid of the thought. Thus, we stay stuck with the idea *'it's my fault and something must be wrong with me'* even as adults.

"Any time a situation in our life triggers the memory of this pain or the idea attached to it, we emotionally regress. Thus, we feel and behave like the little kid who first experienced the pain. In fact, that's precisely what happened when you saw my Lorraine cause our father to feel love. You were twenty-seven years old, but at that moment you regressed to the two-year-old Jill who felt unloved and acted out all your childhood neediness. And you are still doing it, only this time you are doing it with your husband.

"The idea upon which you based all your relationships represents an interpretation made by a two-year-old kid and has absolutely no basis in fact," I concluded. "Do you see that, Jill?" I asked.

"Yes, I do," she replied. "I made some pretty silly decisions based on those unconscious assumptions, didn't I?"

27

"Yes, you did, but you made them when you were in pain and when you were too young to know any better. Even though you repressed the pain to get rid of it, the belief kept working in your life at a subconscious level. That's when your soul decided to create some drama in your life so you would bring it to consciousness again and have the opportunity to choose healing once more.

"You attracted people into your life who would confront you directly with your own pain and make you re-live the original experience through them," I continued.

"That's what Jeff is doing right now. Of course, I am not saying he is doing this consciously. He really isn't. He is probably more perplexed at his own behavior than are you. Remember, this is a soul-to-soul transaction. His soul knows about your original pain and is aware that you will not heal it without going through the experience again."

"Wow!" Jill said, and took a deep breath. She relaxed her body for the first time since we had begun talking about the situation.

"It's certainly a totally different way of looking at things, but do you know what? I feel lighter. It's as if a weight has been lifted off my shoulders just by talking it through with you."

"That's because your energy has shifted," I replied. "Imagine how much of your life-force energy you have had to expend just keeping the story about Dad and Lorraine alive. Plus, imagine the amount of energy required to keep down the feelings of grief and resentment wrapped around the story. The tears you shed earlier enabled you to release a lot of that. And you have just acknowledged that it was all just a made-up story anyway — what a relief that must be. In addition, you've had a lot of energy locked up around Jeff — making him wrong, making yourself wrong, being a victim, and so on. Just being willing to see the whole situation differently enables you to release all that energy and allow it to move through you. No wonder you feel lighter!" I said, and smiled.

"What would have happened if, instead of understanding what was going on underneath the situation with Jeff, I had simply left him?" Jill asked.

"Your soul would have brought in someone else to help you heal," I quickly replied. "But you didn't leave him, did you? You came here instead. You have to understand, this trip was no accident. There are no such things as accidents in this system. You — or rather your soul — created this trip, this opportunity to understand the dynamics of the situation with Jeff. Your soul guided you here. John's soul created a trip at this particular time to make it possible for you to come with him."

"And what about the two Lorraines," Jill wondered. "How did that happen? Surely, that's just a coincidence."

"There are no coincidences in this system either. Just know that your souls, and the souls of some others, conspired to create this situation, and notice how perfect it was that a person named Lorraine was involved in the original occasion and in this one. It couldn't have been a more perfect clue. It's hard to imagine that it wasn't set up somehow, don't you agree?" I said.

"So, what do I do with this now," asked Jill. "It's true that I feel lighter, but what do I do when I go home and see Jeff?"

"There really is very little for you to do," I answered. "From this point on, it's more a question of how you feel inside yourself. Do you understand that you are no longer a victim? Do you understand that Jeff is no longer a persecutor? Do you see that the situation was exactly what you needed and wanted? Do you feel how much that man loves you — at the soul level, I mean?"

"What do you mean?" Jill asked.

"He was willing to do whatever it took to get you to the point where you could look again at your belief about yourself and see that it was untrue. Do you realize how much discomfort he was willing to endure to help you? He is not a cruel man by nature, so it must have been hard for him. Few men could have done that for you while risking losing you in the process. Jeff, or Jeff's soul, truly is an angel for you. When you really understand this, you will feel so grateful to him! Plus, you will stop sending out messages that you are unlovable. You will have the ability to let in love perhaps for the first time in your life. You will have forgiven Jeff, because you will be clear that nothing wrong ever took place. It was perfect in every sense.

"And I promise you this," I continued. "Jeff is already changing as we speak and dropping his bizarre behavior. His soul is already picking up that you have forgiven him and healed your misperception about yourself. As you change your energy, his changes too. You're connected energetically. Physical distance is irrelevant."

Getting back to her question, I said, "So, you won't have to do anything special when you get home. In fact, I want you to promise me that you won't do anything at all when you get back. In particular, do not, under any circumstances, share with Jeff this new way of looking at the situation. I want you to see how everything will be different automatically simply as a consequence of you changing your perception.

"You will feel changed as well," I added. "You will find yourself feeling more peaceful, more centered and more relaxed. You will have a knowingness that will seem strange to Jeff for a while. It will take time for your relationship with him to adjust, and it may still be difficult for a while, but this issue will resolve now," I concluded with conviction.

Jill and I reviewed this new way of looking at her situation many times before she returned home to England. It is always difficult for someone in the middle of an emotional upset to shift into a Radical Forgiveness perspective. In

31

fact, getting to a place where Radical Forgiveness can truly take place often requires a great deal of integration and repetitive reinforcement. To help my sister, I introduced her to some breathing techniques that help release emotion and integrate new ways of being and asked her to complete a Radical Forgiveness worksheet. (See Section Four, Tools For Radical Forgiveness.)

The day she left, Jill obviously was nervous about going back to the situation she had left behind. As she walked down the jetway to her airplane, she looked back and tried to wave confidently, but I knew she was scared that she might lose her newfound understanding and get drawn back into the drama.

Apparently the meeting with Jeff went well. Jill requested that he not question her immediately about what had happened while she was away. She also requested that he give her space for a few days in order to get settled. However, she immediately noticed a difference in him. He was attentive, kind and considerate — more like the Jeff she had known before this whole episode began.

Over the next couple of days, Jill told Jeff she no longer blamed him for anything, nor did she want him to change in any way. She said she had learned that it was she who needed to take responsibility for her own feelings and that she would deal with whatever came up for her in her own way without making him wrong. She did not elaborate at all and did not try to explain herself.

Things went on well for some days after Jill's return home, and Jeff's behavior with his daughter Lorraine changed dramatically. In fact, everything seemed to be getting back to normal with regard to that relationship, but the atmosphere between Jeff and Jill remained tense and their communication limited.

About two weeks later, the situation came to a head. Jill looked at Jeff and said quietly, "I feel like I've lost my best friend."

"So do I," he replied.

For the first time in months they connected. They hugged each other and began to cry. "Let's talk," Jill said. "I've got to tell you what I learned with Colin in America. It's going to sound weird to you at first, but I want to share it with you. You don't have to believe it. I just want you to hear me. Are you willing?"

"I'll do whatever it takes," replied Jeff. "I know something important happened to you there. I want to know what it was. You have changed, and I like what I see. You are not the same person you were when you stepped on the airplane with John. So, tell me what happened."

Jill talked and talked. She explained the dynamics of Radical Forgiveness as best she could in a way Jeff could understand. She felt strong and powerful — sure of herself and her understanding, secure and clear in her mind.

Jeff, a practical man who always is skeptical of anything that cannot be rationally explained, did not resist this time, and he was indeed quite receptive to the ideas that Jill asked him to consider. He voiced openness to the idea that there might be a spiritual world beneath everyday reality and, given that, saw a certain logic in the Radical Forgiveness concept. He didn't accept it totally, but he nevertheless was willing to listen, to consider, and to see how it had changed Jill.

After the discussion, they both felt their love had been rekindled and that their relationship had a good chance of surviving. They made no promises, though, and agreed to keep talking to each other while they watched how their relationship progressed.

It did, indeed, progress quite well. Jeff still fawned over his daughter Lorraine to a degree, but not as much as before. Jill found she cared hardly at all, even when he did behave in this manner. It certainly did not trigger her to regress emotionally and react from old beliefs about herself.

Within a month of their conversation about Radical Forgiveness, all of Jeff's past behavioral pattern with Lorraine stopped. In turn, Lorraine didn't call or visit as often; she got on with her life. Everything slowly returned to normal and Jill and Jeff's relationship began to grow more secure and loving than ever before. Jeff became the kind, sensitive man that he is by nature, Jill became less needy and Lorraine became much happier.

Looking back, had Jill's soul not brought her to Atlanta to create the opportunity for us to have our conversation, I feel sure she and Jeff would have separated. In the grand scheme of things, that would have been all right, too. Jill simply would have found someone else with whom to rec-reate the drama and another opportunity to heal. As it was, she took the opportunity to heal this time and stayed in the relationship.

At the time of writing this book, many years after that cri-sis, they remain together and are very happily married. Like every other couple they continue to create dramas in their lives — but they know now how to see them as healing opportunities and to move through them quickly and with grace.

Postscript: The 'time-line' diagram on the next page depicts Jill's story as a graphic. She found this very helpful in seeing how the original pain of not feeling loved by her father had led to a belief that she was not enough and how, in turn, that belief had played out in her life. You might do the same for yourself if you think you have a similar story running your life.

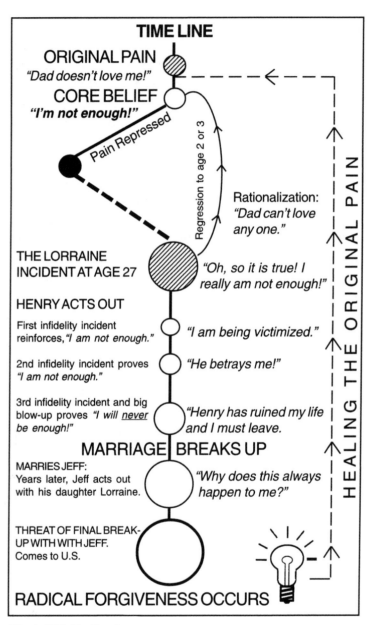

Fig. 1: Jill's Healing Journey

PART TWO

Conversations On Radical Forgiveness

2: Underlying Assumptions

Since all theories are based upon certain assumptions, I think it is important that I lay out what assumptions I have used as my context for the theory and practice of Radical Forgiveness. Before looking at these though, it is worth noting that even the most widely accepted theories are based on assumptions for which there is very little hard evidence.

For example, did you know that little evidence exists to support Darwin's Theory of Evolution? Historically, that theory probably ranks as one of the biggest assumptions ever made. It serves as the basis for biological science and is the very foundation on which much of our accepted scientific *truth* rests. However, the fact that no evidence exists to prove this assumption true does not mean that the theory is not useful. It provides the context for sensible conversation about the history of life and is at least supported, if not proven, by a lot of empirical evidence.

We can say the same thing about the basic assumptions handed down throughout the ages about God, human nature, and the spiritual realm. While there is little hard scientific evidence to support their validity, such assumptions have been handed down to us as *universal truths, or principles,* for centuries and have formed the foundation for many great spiritual traditions throughout the world. They certainly are foundational for Radical Forgiveness. Many of these assumptions are now being proven by physicists to be scientifically well founded.

I have listed my assumptions in the hope that they help you follow the logic of Radical Forgiveness. Each assumption is expanded upon in length at various other places in the book. I refer to them not as truths, nor even beliefs, but as assumptions that I make that, for me, provide some kind of basis for the Radical Forgiveness technology.

My Assumptions:

- We have bodies that die, but we have immortal souls that transcend death. (Therefore death is an illusion.)

- While our bodies and our senses tell us we are separate individuals, we are all **one**. We all individually vibrate as part of a single whole.

- We are *not* human beings having an occasional spiritual experience; rather *we are spiritual beings having a human experience.*

- Vibrationally, we live in two worlds simultaneously:
    1) The World of Divine Truth (Spirit)
    2) The World of Humanity

- We have chosen to fully experience the energy of the World of Humanity simply to magnify, many times over, our appreciation of the beauty of our being part of the **One** in Light and Love, by choosing to experience their direct opposites (fear, separation, darkness) in this world of physicality. This world, therefore, is a spiritual classroom and life is the curriculum. The objective is to awaken to the truth of who we are and return home.

• When we decided to learn and grow by incarnating into the world of humanity, God gave us total **free will** to live the experiment in any way we chose and to find for ourselves the way back home.

• Life is not random. It provides for the purposeful unfoldment of our own Divine plan with opportunities to make choices and decisions in every moment.

• An assumption quite different from the above, and less attractive, is that when we were one with the *All-That-Is*, we experimented with the thought that separation was possible. (The original sin.) We projected that thought; it became our (false) reality — this world — and the Ego (our belief in separation) was born. The Ego now ensures its survival by "protecting" us from our overwhelming guilt, as well as the fear of God's wrath, through the mechanisms of repression and projection. (See Chapter 5.)

• We create our reality through the Law of Cause and Effect. Thoughts are causes that show up in our world as physical effects. Reality is an outplaying of our consciousness. Our world offers a mirror of our beliefs. (See Chapter 8.)

41

- We, at the soul level, get precisely what we need in our lives for our spiritual growth. How we judge what we actually get determines whether we experience life as either painful or joyful.

- Through relationship we grow and learn. Through relationship we heal and are returned to wholeness and truth. We need others to mirror our misperceptions and our projections and to help us bring repressed material to consciousness for healing.

- Through the Law of Resonance, we attract people who resonate with our issues so we can heal them. In that sense they serve as our teachers.

- Physical reality is an illusion created by our five senses. Matter consists of interrelating energy fields vibrating at different frequencies.

Again, if you find yourself unable to accept any of these assumptions, simply disregard them. It will make no difference to the effectiveness of either Radical Forgiveness or the Q-Work tools contained in the Quantum Energy Management System. However, rather than immediately reject them out of hand, why not give them some careful thought and at least remain open to the possibility that is an element of truth in them?

3: Worlds Apart

Wand that we might learn from Jill's story is that things are not always what they seem. What appears to be cruel and nasty behavior on somebody's part might be exactly what we need and have indeed called forth. Situations that appear to be the worst that could possibly befall us may hold the key to our healing something deep within us that keeps us from being happy and prevents our growth. The people who seem to us to be the most troublesome and the least likeable could therefore be our greatest teachers.

If I am right about this, then it follows that whatever appears to be happening is seldom what is truly occurring. Beneath the apparent circumstances of every situation exists a wholly different reality — a different world altogether; a world that we are not privy to except for the occasional glimpse.

Jill's story demonstrates this fact beautifully. On the surface there was the drama of what was happening between her, Jeff and his daughter, Lorraine. It was not pretty. It looked as though Jeff was being cruel and insensitive. It was easy to identify Jill as a victim in the situation and Jeff as the villain. Yet there were enough clues in the situation to lead us to the possibility that something else of a more loving nature was happening — and that it was being orchestrated at the spiritual level.

As the story unfolded, it became obvious that Jill's spiritual intelligence was doing a dance with the souls of Jeff and Lorraine and that the situation being played out was purely for her healing. Moreover, far from being a villain, Jeff was actually a hero, and from that spiritual perspective, had done nothing wrong. He had simply played his part in the drama, as dictated by his own spiritual intelligence, acting in support of Jill's healing at the soul level.

When we shift our perspective to this possibility, we become open to the idea that nothing wrong took place and that in fact there was nothing to forgive. This is precisely the notion that defines Radical Forgiveness. It is also what makes it RADICAL.

If we had asked Jill to apply traditional forgiveness to this situation, we would not have investigated this *'other world'* possibility. We would have taken the evidence of our five senses and used our intellect to come to the conclusion that she had been wronged and badly treated by Jeff and that if she was to forgive him she would have to accept what he did and try her best to 'let bygones be bygones.'

From this we notice that traditional forgiveness takes it as a given that something wrong happened. Radical Forgiveness on the other hand takes the position that NOTHING wrong happened and that consequently, there is nothing to forgive.

44

Different Worlds — Different Perspectives

Radical Forgiveness is different from traditional forgiveness because it is rooted, not in the every day reality of physical form but in the metaphysical reality of the world of Spirit — what I call the World of Divine Truth.

This makes the distinction between Radical and traditional forgiveness very clear, because we can see now that in each case we look through completely different lenses. The lens we are using to view a situation through will determine whether we are using traditional forgiveness or Radical Forgiveness. Each one provides us with a totally different point of view.

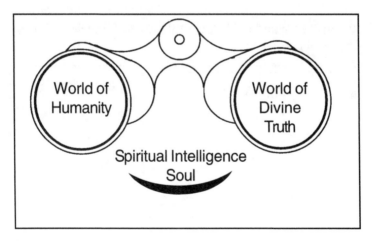

Figure 2: Perspectives On Two Worlds.

But we should not fall into the trap of thinking of it in terms of *either/or.* It is *a both/and* situation. This is because we

45

live with one foot in each world (since we are spiritual beings having a human experience) and can therefore reference situations through either lens or both lenses at the same time. While being fully grounded in the World of Humanity, we remain connected to the World of Divine Truth through our soul, via our spiritual intelligence.

Since the importance of the distinction between these two worlds cannot be overemphasized, some further explanation will be helpful here. The World of Humanity and the World of Divine Truth represent two ends of a vibrational scale. When we vibrate at a low frequency, our bodies become dense and we exist only in the World of Humanity. When we vibrate at a high level, which makes our bodies become lighter, we exist also in the World of Divine Truth. Depending upon our vibration at any moment, we move up and down the scale toward one world or the other.

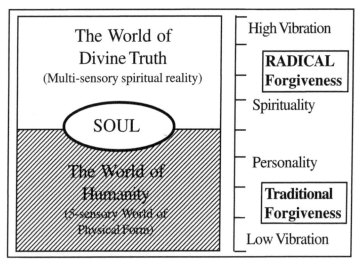

Figure 3. The Existential Chain of Being

The World of Humanity represents the world of objective reality we see as *outside ourselves.* As a world of form, it provides the setting in which we live our everyday human lives, as well as the reality we experience through our five senses. It holds the energy patterns of death, change, fear, limitation, and duality. This world provides us with the environment in which we, as spiritual beings, can experience being human. This means having a physical body and working with (and possibly transcending) a particular energy pattern associated with the World of Humanity that we may have specifically 'come in' to work with.

The World of Divine Truth, on the other hand, has no physical form and already carries the energy pattern of eternal life, immutability, infinite abundance, love, and oneness with God. Even though we cannot perceive this world with our senses, and we scarcely possess the mental capacity to comprehend it, we can get enough of a sense of it to know that it is real. Such activities as prayer, meditation and Radical Forgiveness, all of which raise our vibration, allow us to access the World of Divine Truth.

These *existential realms* differ not in terms of place or time but solely in their vibrational level. The study of quantum physics has proven that all reality consists of energy patterns and that consciousness sustains these energy patterns. Thus, the world of form exists as dense concentrations of energy vibrating at frequencies we can experience through our physical senses. On the other hand, we experience the World of Divine Truth as an inner knowing and an extrasensory awareness.

Because these two worlds exist on the same continuum, we do not live sometimes in one and sometimes in the other. We live in both worlds at the same time. However, which world we experience at any given moment depends upon our awareness of them. Obviously, as human beings our consciousness resonates easily with the World of Humanity. Our senses naturally pull us into that world and convince us that it is real. Though some people are less grounded in the world of objective reality than others, human beings, on the whole, are firmly entrenched at this end of the continuum — which is how it should be.

Our awareness of the World of Divine Truth is limited, and this too appears to be by design. Our soul enters into this world to experience being human — thus our memory and awareness of the World of Divine Truth must be limited to allow us the full experience. We would not be able to take on fully the energies of change, fear, death, limitation, and duality that characterize this world if we knew they were illusory. If we incarnated with this memory, we would deny ourselves the opportunity to transcend these states and *to discover* that they are, indeed, simply illusions. By forgetting who we are when we take on a physical body, we give ourselves the chance to remember that we are spiritual beings having a physical experience.

During a gathering in Atlanta in 1990, I heard Gerald Jampolsky, a well known author, tell a true story about a couple returning home from the hospital after giving birth to their second child.

It is a story that illustrates the fact that we have a true knowing of our connection with God and our own soul but that we forget it fairly quickly after taking on a body. The couple was conscious of the need to include their three-year-old daughter in the celebration of the new baby's homecoming. But they felt perturbed by her insistence that she be allowed to go alone into the room with the baby. To honor her request, yet oversee the situation, they switched on the baby monitor so they could at least hear what was going on, if not see it. What they heard astounded them. The little girl went straight to the crib, looked through the bars at the newborn child, and said, "Baby, tell me about God. I'm beginning to forget."

The soul normally experiences no limitation. However, when it incarnates, the soul creates a personality, or Ego, that carries the particular characteristics it needs for its healing journey and chooses to forget its connection to the World of Divine Truth.

In spite of the veil we lower over the memory of our oneness with God, which the above story suggests might become fully drawn around the age of three, as humans we are not denied a connection to the World of Divine Truth. Our soul carries a vibration that resonates with the World of Divine Truth and connects us to that world.

We can aid this connection through practices like prayer, meditation, breathwork, dancing, and chanting. Through such practices we raise our vibration enough to resonate with that of the World of Divine Truth.

There is evidence to suggest that even this is changing rapidly. Everywhere I go I ask the same question of my workshop participants. *"How many of you are aware of a quickening or a speedup in our spiritual evolution — and that we are being asked by Spirit to move more quickly through our lessons in preparation for a profound shift of some kind?"* There is almost unanimous concurrence. More and more people now talk openly and freely about always being in touch with their 'guidance' and are willing to trust it more each day. The veil between the two worlds is definitely becoming thinner. Radical Forgiveness contributes to this process both at the individual level and at the level of collective awareness.

Yet the two types of forgiveness remain literally worlds apart. They each demand a different way of looking at the world and at life. Clearly, traditional forgiveness offers itself as *a way of living in the world* while Radical Forgiveness is nothing less than *a spiritual path.*

In terms of our capacity to heal ourselves and to evolve spiritually, Radical Forgiveness offers extraordinary potential to transform consciousness, and this potential far exceeds what is possible with traditional forgiveness.

Yet, we must recognize that we all still live in the World of Humanity, and at certain times we will fall short of what we might think of as the spiritual ideal. When we find ourselves immersed in pain, for example, it becomes virtually impossible for us to move into Radical Forgiveness. When we have recently experienced harm at the hand of another, such as when we have just been raped, we cannot be expected to accept, in that moment, that the experience was something we wanted and that it represents the unfoldment of a Divine plan. We will not have the receptivity necessary to entertain that idea. It can only come later in moments of quiet reflection, not in the heat of anger and in the immediate aftermath of a trauma.

But then again, we must continually remind ourselves that what we have created IS the spiritual ideal; that we have created circumstances in our lives that help us grow and learn; that the lessons we need to learn are contained in the situation and that the only way to obtain the growth from the experience is to go *through* it.

The choice we have in this is not so much as to whether to have the experience (Spirit decides this for us), but how long we are going to hang out in victim consciousness because of it. Should we choose to quickly let go of the victim it is comforting to know that we have a technology that will make that happen. Traditional forgiveness by contrast has little to offer in this regard.

Summary:

- **Traditional Forgiveness** is firmly rooted in the World of Humanity. In the same way that the World of Humanity holds the energy of duality, so traditional forgiveness polarizes and judges everything as either good or bad, right or wrong. *Radical Forgiveness takes the view that there is no right/wrong or good/bad. Only our thinking makes it so.*

- **Traditional Forgiveness** always begins with the assumption that something wrong took place, and someone 'did something' to someone else. The victim archetype remains operative. *Radical Forgiveness begins with the belief that nothing wrong happened, and there are no victims in any situation.*

- **Traditional Forgiveness** is effective to the extent that it calls upon the highest human virtues, such as compassion, tolerance, kindness, mercy, and humility. These qualities point towards forgiveness and have healing potential. However, in and of themselves, they are not forgiveness. *Radical Forgiveness is no different in this regard since it also calls for these same virtues to be present in the process.*

- **Traditional Forgiveness** depends entirely upon our own capacity to feel compassion, so it is limited in this regard. No matter how much compassion or tolerance we muster for someone like Hitler, and no matter how much we empathize with the pain of his upbringing, nothing enables us to forgive him (using traditional forgiveness) for the mass murder of six million Jews. *Radical Forgiveness has no limits whatsoever and is completely unconditional. If Radical Forgiveness cannot forgive Hitler, it can forgive nobody. Like unconditional love, it's all or nothing.*

• With **Traditional Forgiveness**, the Ego and our personality-self call the shots. Hence, the problem always appears 'out-there' with someone else. *With Radical Forgiveness, the finger points the other way — the problem lies 'in here,' with me.*

• **Traditional Forgiveness** believes in the reality of the physical world, in the complete integrity of 'what happens' and always tries to 'figure it all out' and thus, control the situation. *Radical Forgiveness recognizes the illusion, sees that what happened was just a story and responds by surrendering to the perfection of the situation.*

• **Traditional Forgiveness** does not factor in the notion of a spiritual mission and maintains its belief in, and fear of, death. *Radical Forgiveness sees death as an illusion and takes the view that life is eternal.*

• **Traditional Forgiveness** views life as a problem to be solved or punishment to be avoided. It experiences life as a random set of circumstances that just happen to us for no reason — thus, the origin of the popular bumper sticker, 'S__ happens!' *Radical Forgiveness sees life as entirely purposeful and motivated by love.*

53

- **Traditional Forgiveness** recognizes the inherent imperfection of human beings but fails to see the *perfection in the imperfection.* It cannot resolve that paradox. *Radical Forgiveness exemplifies that paradox.*

- **Traditional Forgiveness** can carry a high vibration similar to Radical Forgiveness when calling upon some of the highest of human virtues, like kindness, humility, compassion, patience, and tolerance. The portal through which we begin the journey of raising our vibration to connect with the world of Divine Truth and experience **Radical Forgiveness** is the open heart.

- **Traditional Forgiveness,** when of a very high vibration, recognizes the profundity of the spiritual insight that we *all* are imperfect and that imperfection characterizes the nature of humanity. When we look at a wrongdoer through these eyes, we can say in all humility and with tolerance and compassion, "There, but for the Grace of God, go I." We own that we, too, are completely capable of whatever the accused person has done. If we are acquainted with our shadow-self, we know that we all have within us the potential to cause harm, to murder, to rape, to abuse children, and to annihilate six million people. This knowledge allows us to call forth our humility and makes us kind and merciful not only to the accused but to ourselves, for in them we recognize our own inherent imperfection, our own shadow. This recognition brings us very close to actually taking back that which we projected — the vital first step in Radical Forgiveness. *Radical Forgiveness also lovingly sees*

54

the imperfection inherent in human beings but sees the perfection in the imperfection.

- **Radical Forgiveness** recognizes that forgiveness cannot be willed or bestowed. We must *be willing* to forgive and to give the situation over to our Higher Power. Forgiveness of any kind comes not from effort but from being open to experiencing it.

TRADITIONAL FORGIVENESS	vs.	RADICAL FORGIVENESS
World of Humanity (Ego)	vs.	World of Divine Truth (Spirit)
Low vibratory rate	vs.	High vibratory rate
Something wrong happened	vs.	Nothing wrong happened
Judgment based	vs.	Judgment and blame free
Past orientation	vs.	Present time orientation
Need to figure it all out	vs.	Surrendering to what is as is
Victim consciousness	vs.	Grace consciousness
Judges human imperfection	vs.	Accepts human imperfection
What happened did (true)	vs.	Symbolic meaning of it (truth)
Physical reality only	vs.	Metaphysical realities
Problem is still 'out there'	vs.	Problem is with me (my error)
Letting go of resentment	vs.	Embracing the resentment
You and I are separate	vs.	You and I are ONE
'Shit happens'	vs.	There are no accidents
Life is random events	vs.	Life is purposeful
Personality (ego) in control	vs.	Soul following a divine plan
Reality is what happens	vs.	Reality is what we create
Death is real	vs.	Death is an illusion

Fig. 4: Distinctions between Traditional and Radical Forgiveness

4: Accountability

It needs to be clearly understood that Radical Forgiveness does not relieve us from responsibility in this world. We are spiritual beings having a human experience in a world governed by both physical and man-made laws, and as such, we are necessarily held to account for all our actions. That is an inherent part of the human experience which cannot be avoided.

In other words, when we create circumstances that hurt other people, we must accept that in the World of Humanity there are consequences for such actions. While, from a Radical Forgiveness standpoint, we would say that all parties involved in the situation are getting what they need, it is also true that experiencing the consequences, like going to jail, being fined, being shamed and condemned is all part of the lesson and is perfect once again in that spiritual context.

I am often asked whether, in a situation where someone has done us harm and where the normal reaction would be to seek redress through the courts, a forgiving person would actually take that course of action? The answer is, "*Yes.*" We live in the World of Humanity which operates within the parameters of the Law of Cause and Effect.

This states that for every action there is a correspondingly equal reaction. Thus, early on we learn that our actions have consequences. If we were never held accountable for our actions, forgiveness would be meaningless and valueless. With no accountability put upon us, it would appear as if, no matter what we did, no one cared. Such an action or attitude offers no compassion whatsoever. For instance, children always interpret *rightful* parental discipline applied appropriately as caring and loving. Conversely, they interpret being given total license by their parents as non-caring. Children know.

However, the extent to which we respond to other people's actions with a sense of righteous indignation, grievance, revenge, and resentment, rather than with a genuine desire to balance the scales with regard to principles of fairness, freedom, and respect for others, determines our level of forgiveness. Righteousness and revenge lower our vibration. Conversely, defense of principles and acting with integrity raises our vibration. The higher the vibration, the closer we come to Divine Truth and the more able we are to forgive radically.

I recently heard bestselling author Alan Cohen tell a story that illustrates this point well. A friend of his once got involved in circumstances that resulted in a girl's death. For her wrongful death, he was imprisoned for many years. He accepted the responsibility for what had happened and behaved in every way as a model prisoner. However, the girl's father, a rich and influential man with friends in high places, made a vow to keep this man locked up for as many years as possible. So, every time this man became eligible for parole, the girl's father spent a great deal of time and money pulling every political string possible to make sure parole was denied. After numerous such occurrences, Cohen asked his friend how he felt about being denied parole because of this man's efforts to keep him in prison. The man said he forgave the girl's father every day of his life and prayed for him, because he realized that it was the father who was in prison, not himself.

In truth, the father who was unable to get beyond his rage, sadness, and grief, was controlled by his need for revenge. He could not escape the prison of his own victimhood. Even traditional forgiveness was beyond him. Cohen's friend, on the other hand, refused to be a victim and saw love as the only possibility. His vibration was higher, and he was able to practice Radical Forgiveness.

Getting back to the issue of whether or not to seek redress through the courts, we should seek to make others accountable for their actions. Remember, though, that once we decide to sue, we must, as they say in AA, "pray for the S.O.B.," and for ourselves. (By the way, we do not have to like someone to forgive them!) In other words, we turn the matter over to our Higher Power. We recognize that Divine Love operates in every situation and that each person receives exactly what they want. We recognize that perfection always resides somewhere in the situation, even if it is not apparent at the time.

I had occasion to experience this myself when I had just completed this book and was looking around for someone to help me market it. A friend recommended someone, so my wife JoAnna and I went to see her. She seemed OK, and I had no reason to doubt her skill or integrity. However — it's funny how the Universe works — the deadline for getting the title into 'Books in Print,' was the next day. This is the reference book that bookstores use for ordering so it was important to get in then — or miss a whole year. But that also meant I was rushed into signing a contract with this woman. In addition, it meant coming up with $4,000, which is what she wanted up-front, as well as 15% of the book sales. We didn't have $4,000 but JoAnna somehow came up with $2,900. We would pay the rest in monthly installments. So we signed. Though rushed into it, I was pleased that I had delegated that part of the project.

Well, as the months went by, and well after my book was published, I noticed that I was still having to do a lot of what I thought I had contracted with her to do. I was booking all my own book signings, sending books to reviewers and so on. I wasn't seeing any results from her efforts at all. I kept my eye on it, but after a while I confronted her. It turned out that she had hardly done a thing. Of course she denied it and defended herself, but when I demanded to see letters and evidence of activity, there was nothing. I fired her, voided the contract for nonperformance, and demanded my money back. Of course, she refused. So I started court proceedings to recoup the money.

As you can imagine, I was pretty upset. I was stuck where all people who imagine themselves victimized go, in "victimland!" And I was totally unconscious. I had my victim story all made up and took every opportunity to share it with anyone who would listen. As far as I was concerned, she stole that money from me, and I needed to get even. I was well and truly stuck, and I stayed that way for several weeks. And I was supposed to be *Mr. Forgiveness!*

Fortunately, a friend who had come to my first workshop many years ago came to dinner. When I told her my story, her response was, "Well, have you done a worksheet around this?" Of course, I hadn't. It was the thing furthest from my mind. "No I haven't done a worksheet," I replied feeling very angry. "Don't you think you should?" Lucie asked. "No, I don't want to do an darn worksheet," I shouted.

Then JoAnna chimed in. "Well, it's your worksheet. You ought to practice what you preach!" That did it. Feeling cornered I stomped upstairs to get one, but I was angry. I knew, and so did they, that I was doing it under protest. It was the last thing in the world I wanted to do, but they wouldn't let me off the hook. I did each step in a huff and with little or no commitment to the process.

Then all of a sudden, as I got about half way through, I had to read the statement — "I release the need to blame and the need to be right." That's when it hit me. *The need to be right!* All of a sudden it flashed before me what I was trying to be right about. I had a core belief that I always had to do everything myself! I saw that this incident was just another out-playing of that belief. All the other times I had unconsciously created being let down that way flashed before my eyes. I then saw and fully understood that this woman was

61

supporting me in becoming acquainted with my toxic belief so I could release it and open myself to greater abundance.

Suddenly, all my anger evaporated, and I saw how I had shut myself off from the very things I believed in and was teaching. I felt very ashamed. But at least I was conscious again. I could now see that this woman was an *'angel of healing'* for me, and I switched from feeling anger and resentment to feeling profound gratitude and love for her.

Besides having that wonderful healing, it was a very powerful and humbling lesson in how easy it is to go unconscious about spiritual law and how quickly your Ego will suck you into a drama and keep you there. It was a frightening demonstration of the power of my Ego to separate me from my Source and from everything I know to be true. It was also a powerful demonstration of why we need spiritual friends who will support us by not buying into our victim story and being prepared to challenge us on it.

However, the question you are probably asking is, having realized that she was a healing angel for me, did I cancel the court case against her? Well, I can tell you, I agonized over this.

I recognized that, even though I now saw the truth from the perspective of the World of Divine Truth, the situation itself was deeply grounded in the World of Humanity. So I offered to mediate twice, and she refused on both occasions.

I therefore went ahead with the court case, reasoning that her soul needed to have that experience, otherwise it would have taken her out of it when I offered to mediate. But I went into it with my heart open and with the intention that the right and perfect outcome would ensue. The court found in my favor and I got a judgment against her for most of the $4,000. I never got the money, but that didn't matter. The point was that we had trusted the process and had done what seemed to be necessary at the time.

And the truth is, it wouldn't have mattered which way I decided. Spirit would have sorted it out some other way, and it all would have worked out OK in the end — as it always does. The idea that our decisions matter in the overall scheme of things is just our Ego trying to make us feel separate and special. The Universe has everything handled no matter what we decide. But how we make those decisions — whether from love or fear, greed or generosity, false pride or humility, dishonesty or integrity — matters to us personally because each decision we make affects our vibration.

Another situation I am often asked to address is when one becomes aware of a child being abused. The question raised is that if we assume that the child's spiritual growth is being supported by this experience, should we take action or not, since to interfere would be to deny the child's soul its growth experience? My answer is always that, as human beings, we must do what it is right according to our present awareness of right and wrong — as defined in human law. So we act accordingly while at the same time knowing that, in spiritual law, nothing wrong is taking place. Naturally then, we would

63

intervene. As human beings, we could not do otherwise. But our intervention is not wrong or right either, because either way Spirit has it handled.

My reasoning is that if it were in the best interests of the child's soul for there to be no intervention, Spirit would arrange things in such a way as to prevent it. In other words, if I were not supposed to intervene, Spirit would keep me unaware of the situation. Conversely, if Spirit makes me aware of the situation, I assume it has no problem with my intervening. In the end, it is not even my decision.

When I do intervene, however, I do it free of judgment and the need to blame anyone. I just do it, knowing that the Universe set the whole thing up for a reason and that there is a perfection in there somewhere.

5: The Mechanisms of the Ego

In matters of a spiritual nature, it is seldom long before the conversation turns to the Ego. Radical Forgiveness is no exception since the Ego does seem to play a central role. So, what constitutes the Ego and what role does it play in Radical Forgiveness?

I feel that there are at least two ways of answering this question. The first casts the Ego as our enemy, while the second sees it as our friend.

The *Ego-As-Enemy* viewpoint makes the Ego responsible for keeping us separated from Source out of self interest for its own survival. Consequently it is our spiritual enemy and we are at war with it. Many spiritual disciplines take this as their central idea and demand that the Ego must be dropped or transcended as a prerequisite for spiritual growth.

The *Ego-As-Friend* model sees the Ego as being the part of our own soul — a part that acts as our loving guide for this human experience.

I prefer to think that there is truth in both of these ideas even though at first blush they seem to be incompatible.

Let me explain each in turn, as I have come to understand them for myself, so you can make up your own mind.

1. Ego As The Enemy:

In this model the Ego is said to exist as a deeply-held set of beliefs about who we are in relationship to Spirit, formed when we experimented with the thought of separation from the Divine Source. In fact, we could say that the Ego is the belief that separation actually occurred.

At the moment of separation, so the story goes, the Ego had us believe that God had become very angry about our experiment. This immediately created enormous guilt within us. The Ego then elaborated on its story by telling us that God would get even and punish us severely for our great sin. So great was the guilt and the terror created in us by the belief that this story was true, we had no choice but to repress these emotions deep in our unconscious mind. This spared us from the conscious awareness of them.

This tactic worked quite well, yet we retained a great fear that the feelings might rise once again. To remedy this problem, the Ego developed a new belief — that the guilt lay with someone else rather than within ourselves. In other words, we began projecting our guilt on to other people so we could be rid of it entirely. They became our *scapegoats*. Then, to ensure that the guilt stayed with them, we became angry with them and kept up a continuous attack on them. *(For more detailed information on denial and projection, see Chapter Seven).*

Herein lies the origin of the victim archetype and the human race's continual need to attack and to defend against each other. After attacking the people onto whom we projected our guilt, we fear them attacking us in return. So, we create strong defenses to protect ourselves and what we see as our complete innocence. At some level we know we are guilty, so the more we defend against the attack the more we reinforce our guilt. Thus, we must constantly find people to hate, to criticize, to judge, to attack, and to make wrong simply so we can feel better about ourselves. This dynamic constantly reinforces the Ego's belief system, and in this manner, the Ego ensures its own survival.

Using this behavior pattern as a reference, we can now see why, throughout history, human beings have had such a high investment in their anger and such a high need to break the world into victims and persecutors, villains and heroes, victors and vanquished, winners and losers.

Furthermore, the perception we have of a *we/they* world reflects our own internal split between the Ego on the one hand, which is the belief in separation, fear, punishment and death; and Spirit on the other, which is the knowledge of love and eternal life. We project this division onto the physical world by always seeing the enemy as *out there,* rather than within ourselves.

While all belief systems quickly become resistant to change the Ego is no ordinary belief system in this regard. It is extremely resistant to change. It holds incredible power in our unconscious mind and carries an enormous block of votes when it comes to making decisions about who we think we are. This belief system is so powerful that it appears to be an entity in its own right — and we have named it the Ego.

We have become trapped in the belief of separation to such a degree that it has become our reality. We have been living the myth of separation for eons, making real the idea that we chose separation by naming it the original sin.

In actuality, no separation ever occurred. We are as much a part of God as we always were. We are spiritual beings having a human experience, remember? Consequently there is no such thing as original sin in this sense.

Anyway, contrary to what the Ego would have us believe, the truth is that we actually come to the physical plane with God's blessing and His unconditional love. God always will honor our free will and our choices at the highest level and will offer no Divine intervention — unless asked. Christians will ask through Jesus, but I believe we can also ask directly for such assistance through doing Radical Forgiveness.. This is because in the process, you demonstrate to that you have seen beyond the Ego and glimpsed the truth — that only love is real — and that we are all One with God including those who seemed at first to be our enemy.

2. The Ego As Loving Guide:

This other, more friendly way of looking at the Ego — which I find equally tenable — holds that far from being our enemy, the Ego is a part of our soul; a part that splits off to play a guidance role in the World of Humanity in absolutely perfect and purposeful opposition to the Higher Self. That role is to provide the anchor in the World of Humanity that would fully test our ability to be a spiritual being having a truly human experience. The only value in having the human experience is precisely to experience such things as the Ego provides: belief in duality, separateness and fear. Furthermore, that we need to experience them fully at the feeling level in order for us to wake up and remember that the opposites are true.

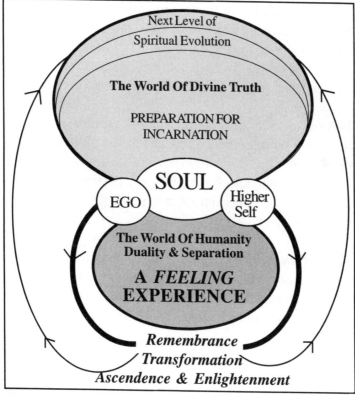

Fig. 5. The Soul's Journey

Our Ego then, in this model, is the guide that will take us on all these journeys into the illusion and try to teach us many false lessons that will keep us stuck in the illusion. But it does so, not out of malice nor even for the sake of its own survival, but because it loves us and knows that we need this experience for our spiritual growth.

But the Ego does not do this alone. The Higher Self is our other guide who waits patiently while we journey into the illusion with the Ego until we are ready to hear the truth. It is through the gentle whispers of the Higher Self that we wake up, bit by bit, until we finally remember who we are and go home. That's what transformation is, and enlightenment too. This is our Soul's journey while in physical form. And there exists no short cut. Without both the Ego and the Higher Self working their magic, we simply wouldn't get there.

I invite you to consider both definitions to be true at the same time. My sense is that the first one is true in terms of it explaining our initial descent into physical form and how we came to see that event (falsely) in retrospect, but that the second is grounded in a deeper truth, namely, that there exists within us no separation of any kind.

Maybe they are two different things, I don't know. It really doesn't matter. Each definition helps me to make sense of this human experience in terms of spiritual truth and I trust they will do the same for you.

6: Hideouts and Scapegoats

U nderstanding the role that the twin psychological ego-defense mechanisms of repression and projection play in how we heal relationships is essential to the concept of Radical Forgiveness. A closer inspection of the mechanisms of each might therefore be helpful.

Operating together, repression and projection wreak havoc upon our relationships and our lives. Together they create and maintain the victim archetype. Understanding how they work enables us to counteract the Ego's use of them to keep us separated from each other and from God.

1. Repression

Operating as a normal psychological defense mechanism, repression occurs when feelings like terror, guilt or rage become so overwhelming that the mind simply blocks them from conscious awareness entirely. This makes repression a powerful mental safety device, for without this blocking mechanism we easily could go mad. It works so effectively that absolutely no memory of the feelings, or the event which precipitated them remain — totally blocked out of conscious awareness for days, weeks or years — sometimes even for the rest of the lifetime.

Suppression:

Repression should not be confused with this other, similar but less severe, defense mechanism. Suppression occurs when we *consciously* refuse to acknowledge emotions that we do not want to feel or express. Though we know they are there, we try to push, or *stuff* them away and refuse to deal with them. However, continued denial of them for long periods of time may lead to a *numbness* equivalent to them becoming repressed.

Repressed Guilt and Shame

Guilt is a universal human experience. Deep in our unconscious mind we have such overwhelming guilt and shame about the thought, albeit not true, that we separated from God (the original sin), that we have no choice but to repress this feeling. We absolutely could not handle these emotions otherwise.

Please note that guilt and shame are not the same. We feel guilt when we feel we have *done* wrong. Shame takes us to a deeper level of guilt where we have a sense of actually *being* wrong. With shame, the Ego makes us feel inherently wrong at the very core of our being. No shame or guilt is as deep seated as the shame of the original sin, the central, but entirely false, plank of the Ego's belief system.

Shame Blocks Energy

Young children can be easily shamed, say, when they wet themselves, get an erection, show anger, act shy, and so on. While these may be natural occurrences, the children nevertheless feel the shame, and the cumulative effects of this feeling can become overwhelming. Consequently, they repress their shame, but it remains in the unconscious mind as well as in the body. It becomes locked into their system at the cellular level and becomes an energy block in the body. If left unresolved for too long, this block gives rise to either mental/emotional problems or physical problems or both. Repressed emotion now is recognized by many researchers to be one of the principal causes of cancer.

Repressed Feelings

A large trauma, such as the death of a parent, can cause a child to repress emotion. Likewise, something seemingly insignificant, such as a casual critical remark interpreted as meaningful, or an event incorrectly assumed to be his/her fault, can cause emotions to be repressed. For example, children nearly always interpret a divorce as their fault. Research suggests that children remember conversations their parents had while they were still in the womb. A discussion about an unwanted pregnancy before birth can lead to a child's feelings of being unwanted and fear of being abandoned. Such feelings would be repressed even at such an early time in the child's life.

Generational Guilt

Groups and even nationalities commonly repress accumulated generational guilt. Without doubt, this is the case now with black and white Americans over slavery. The racial problems we now experience in America all stem from the unresolved and repressed guilt within white people and unresolved and repressed rage in the blacks.

The Dark Side

We also experience intense shame over aspects of ourselves that we dislike and, therefore, disown. Carl Jung, the famous Swiss psychiatrist, referred to this as our *shadow*, because it represents the dark side of ourselves, the part that we do not want to see or to have seen. This part of ourselves could kill another human being, knows we could have taken part in the killing of six million Jews had we been German during that time, knows we might have owned and brutalized slaves had we been born white in the South before the Civil War, could hurt or rape someone, is greedy or avaricious, is rageful and vengeful, or is in some other way deviant or unacceptable. Any such characteristic of ourselves, or area of our lives that brings us feelings of shame, we classify as our shadow and then repress it.

Sitting On a Volcano

Repressing this kind of energy is like sitting on a volcano! We never know when our strength will give out, thus allowing the lava (shadow) to spurt forth and wreak havoc on our world. This explains why we need to bring in a scapegoat on whom we can project all that shame. That way we can be free of it, at least temporarily.

2. Projection

Even when we have repressed the feelings and/or memories associated with a life event, we know, on an unconscious level, that the shame, guilt or self-criticism associated with it remains with us. So, we attempt to rid ourselves of that pain by *taking it out* of ourselves and transferring it on to someone, or something, else *outside* of ourselves. This projection process allows us to forget we ever possessed such feelings.

Fig. 6: Projecting Our Repressed Shame

Once we project what we do not want to own onto someone else, we see them, rather than us, possessing those qualities. So, if we repress our guilt and then project it, we make that person the wrong one. If we repress our anger and then project it, we see them as the angry one. We can accuse them of all the things we feared we would be accused of ourselves. No wonder we feel so relieved when we project! In so doing, we make someone else responsible for everything terrible that happens to us or for what we see as negative about ourselves. Then, we can demand that they be punished, so we can feel even more righteous and safe from attack.

This explains why we love to watch the news on television. The news provides us with an opportunity to project all our guilt and shame on the murderers, rapists, corrupt politicians, and other *bad* people we see on the screen. After doing so, we can go to bed feeling okay about ourselves. The news, and all the other television programs that feature *bad* people and situations, endlessly provides us with convenient scapegoats upon whom to project.

Recognize When You're Projecting

As soon as you find yourself judging someone, you know you are projecting. Anger serves as the constant companion of projection, for the Ego uses this emotion in its attempt to justify the projection of guilt. Whenever you get angry, you also know you are projecting your own guilt.

What you find so objectionable about another person simply serves as a reflection of that part of you that you have rejected and denied in yourself (your shadow) and projected onto them instead. If this was not so, you would not be upset.

This concept — ***what we attack and judge in others is really what we condemn in ourselves*** — is the central idea behind Radical Forgiveness and the key to our own soul-level healing.

Resonance

We feel victimized by other people precisely because they resonate with our own guilt, anger, fear, or rage. (See next chapter.) It feels like they are *doing something to us* to make us angry. When we own that the feelings begin with us, not with them, we can drop the need to feel victimized.

The Attack/Defense Cycle

Though repression and projection are meant as temporary relief valves for the psyche, the Ego co-opted them as the means to maintain itself. Remember, the Ego simply consists of a set of beliefs, the central one being that we are separate from God. Following from that belief comes the belief that God is after us and when he catches us he will punish us severely. The Ego uses the dynamics of repression and projection to hide these beliefs, as well as the guilt and fear that accompanies them, from our consciousness. Hence, repression and projection become a permanent way of being for us. Our whole life revolves around our continual repression, denial and projection, all of which are maintained in perpetuity by the never-ending fear/attack and defense/attack cycles. This provides a perfect recipe for continual internal conflict.

The Drive For Wholeness

Fortunately, in spite of the incredible efficiency of repression and projection, the innate drive for wholeness emanating from our souls possesses more power than the Ego.

This drive for wholeness originates from that part of us that knows the truth and is not content to deny it and project it. This part, the soul, which cries out for a return to love, carries the same energy that creates our opportunities for learning and for healing — the energy of Radical Forgiveness.

Fear Of Intimacy

Every person we meet offers us the opportunity to choose between projection or forgiveness, union or separation. However, the more intimate we become with someone and the closer they get to our true self, the more likely it becomes that they will learn the guilty truth about us. This possibility of being *discovered* creates enormous fear inside us — and the temptation to project becomes almost irresistible. At this point, the honeymoon is over. The fear of intimacy becomes so strong that the relationship is likely to fall apart. Most do.

All Relationships Are For Healing

To move forward and succeed, we must understand this phenomenon and use Radical Forgiveness to stay in the relationship and to fulfill its true spiritual purpose — which is to heal the people involved.

As we saw in Jill's Story, Radical Forgiveness can certainly save marriages! However, this is not necessarily the goal. If the purpose of the relationship has been fulfilled, which is to say that the people are healed, the relationship may need to dissolve naturally and peacefully.

7: Attraction & Resonance

As we saw in the previous chapter, we project our guilt and anger onto people who have the capacity to *resonate* with our feelings, and such people become convenient scapegoats.

Just as a radio station uses a certain frequency to broadcast its programs, so our emotions (energy in motion) vibrate at certain frequencies. People who resonate with our feelings vibrate at that same rate and are likely to have a similar emotion pattern to our own - either the same or opposite - which they then mirror back to us.

Our core beliefs also have a certain frequency. By speaking them aloud, we give our beliefs even more energy, and they take on a causal quality in the Universe. Thus, our spoken beliefs cause effects in our world. In addition, other people *resonate* with the energetic frequency of that belief. In other words, they vibrate sympathetically at the same rate with it. When they do so, they are attracted into our lives to mirror our beliefs back to us. That gives us a chance to look at, and if necessary, to change our minds about that belief. It is not only negative beliefs that get mirrored back to us, either. For example, if we are loving and trusting, we will tend to attract people into our lives who are likewise trustworthy and nurturing.

Recall from Part 1 that my sister, Jill, had a belief that she would never be enough for any man. This belief resonated with a man who was a sexual addict. He provided the ideal partner for her, because he supported her belief by continually having sex with other women, thus showing her she was *not enough* for him. She did not make the connection in that relationship and, consequently, did not heal the pain that created this belief in the first place. So, she found another man (Jeff) who resonated with her belief. He supported her belief differently by using his own issue of co-dependence with his daughter, Lorraine, as the catalyst. In this situation, she saw the connection and realized that he was mirroring her belief that she was not enough, and both of them healed.

If you want to know what you dislike about yourself and have likely disowned, simply look at what annoys you about the people who come into your life. Look into the mirror they provide. If you seem to attract a lot of angry people into your life, you probably have not dealt with some anger of your own. If people seem to withhold love from you, some part of you is unwilling to give love. If people seem to steal things from you, part of you behaves dishonestly or feels dishonest. If people betray you, maybe you have betrayed someone in the past.

Look at the issues that upset you, too. If abortion really makes you mad maybe a part of you shows little reverence for life in other ways, or a part of you knows it could abuse a child. If you are passionately against homosexuality, maybe you cannot accept the part of you that sometimes feels homosexually inclined.

Hall of Mirrors

The reflection does not always appear that readily or as simply. For example, sometimes we do not identify with the specific behavior as much as we do with the underlying meaning it holds for us. A man who gets angry about his wife's overeating and obesity may not be resonating with any personal tendency to overeat; instead, he might be resonating with her use of food to avoid dealing with emotional problems, because it mirrors his tendency to run away from his own emotional problems. Clearly, seeing what others mirror for us can become like looking at the myriad of distorted images in a hall of mirrors.

Automatic Reversal of Projection

The beauty of Radical Forgiveness lies in the fact that it does not require that we recognize what we project. We simply forgive the person for what is happening at the time. In doing so, we automatically undo the projection no matter how complicated the situation. The reason for this is simple in that the person represents the original pain that caused us to project in the first place. As we forgive him/her we clear that original pain. Moreover, no matter what we see as our problems, only one basic problem actually exists for any of us — our guilt about separating from God. All other problems derive from this original one.

Ironically, the people who seem to upset us the most are those who, at the soul level, love and support us the most. Almost always, and often at great expense to themselves in terms of their own discomfort, these individuals try to

81

teach us something about ourselves and to encourage us to move towards healing. Remember, this is not a personality-to-personality exchange. In fact, more than likely the personalities of these individuals clash terribly. Instead, the souls of each player set up the scenario in the hope that the person will eventually see their issue and heal.

Don't Take Life So Personally

Who comes into our lives to help us accomplish this task is actually irrelevant. If one particular person does not take the job, somebody else will. The tragedy is that, as the victim, we seldom understand this. We imagine that we just happened to be the unlucky recipient of a particular person's harmful behavior. It does not occur to us that we might have (at the soul level) attracted the person and the situation to ourselves for a reason, and that had it not been this person, it simply would have been someone else. We mistakenly feel that but for this person we would not have had the problem. In other words, we see the problem as entirely with the other person, whom we now feel justified in hating and resenting for *causing* us pain and unhappiness.

Blaming Our Parents

We often hear this type of blame when people talk about their parents. "If I'd had different parents, I'd be whole and complete today," people say. Wrong. They could have chosen a different set of parents, that's true; but the new set would have given them the exact same experience, because that's what their soul wanted.

Repeating Relationship Patterns

When we see ourselves as victims, we think only about killing the messenger. We miss the message. This explains why people today go from marriage to marriage recreating the same relationship dynamic each time. They do not get the message with the first spouse, so they go on to another who continues trying to relay the message the last spouse tried to relay.

Co-dependency And Mutual Projection

We also find others onto whom we project our own self-hatred who will not only accept it but reciprocate by projecting theirs back onto us. We call this kind of agreement a co-dependent or addictive relationship. That special someone compensates for what we feel is missing in ourselves by continually telling us we are okay, so we avoid feeling our shame about who we are. We do the same thing for them in return, thus both people learn to manipulate each other with highly conditional love based on the underlying guilt. (The stereotypical Jewish Mother is a wonderful example of this archetype.) The moment the other person withdraws approval, we are forced to confront our guilt and self-hatred again, and everything collapses. Love turns immediately into hate, and each partner attacks the other. This explains why we see so many faltering relationships, that once seemed supportive and loving, turn into a cauldron of hate almost instantaneously.

8: Cause & Effect

Central to the idea that we create our own reality is the Law of Cause and Effect. This states that every action has an equal reaction. Therefore, every cause must have an effect, and every effect must have a cause. Since thoughts are causal in nature, every thought has an effect in the world. In other words, we — unconsciously for the most part — create our world, the world of humanity, with our thoughts.

When we vibrate at a high frequency, such as when we pray, meditate or contemplate, we can create consciously and intentionally through thought. Most of the time, however, we do so quite unconsciously. Individual random thoughts do not carry a lot of energy, so they create a relatively small effect. However, thoughts accompanied by larger amounts of energy, especially emotional or creative energy, have a much larger effect in the world. Thus, they play a larger hand in creating our reality.

When a thought gathers sufficient energy to become a belief, it has an even greater effect in the world. It becomes an operating principle in our lives, and we then create effects — circumstances, situations, even physical events that hold true to that belief. What we believe about the world is how it always will be for us.

Acceptance of the principle that thought is creative is fundamental to an understanding of Radical Forgiveness, for it allows us to see that what turns up in our lives represents what we have created with our thoughts and our beliefs. It allows us to see that we simply are projecting all our thoughts and beliefs about *the way things are* onto the world.

Projecting the Illusion

Metaphorically, we run a movie, called **Reality**, through our mind (the projector), and we project it *out there*.

Fig. 7: Projecting Our Own Reality

Once we understand that what we call reality is just our projections, instead of blaming others we can begin to take responsibility for what we have created with our thoughts. When we change our perception and drop our attachment to our belief that what appears on the screen represents reality, we experience Radical Forgiveness.

86

Consciousness Determines What Happens

While it may seem difficult to see the principle of cause and effect operating in our lives, it becomes apparent when we trace back from what is occurring. In other words, if you want to know your beliefs, just look at what is happening. That will tell you what you are projecting. For example, if you keep getting attacked or disasters keep happening to you, the likelihood is that you believe the world is inherently an unsafe place. You are creating these events to prove that you are right about that and people are supporting you in this belief by appearing to you to behave in a threatening or dangerous manner.

Some friends of mine have a spiritual conference center in the mountains of North Carolina. Werner, being of a prudent nature, thought he and his wife, Jean, should have insurance to protect their buildings against fire, storm damage and the frequent tornadoes that come through each season. Jean was very much against the idea. She felt having such insurance would clearly indicate to the Universe that they did not trust in their safety. Now, I am not advocating this, but they decided against purchasing the insurance.

The following year, a huge storm hit their very mountain and devastated the area. Thousands of trees were uprooted and thrown down. When my wife and I drove up to visit them two weeks later, we couldn't believe our eyes. It looked like a war zone. They had obviously been obliged to cut their way out. The storm had happened while 36 people were at the center attending a conference, and they were unable to leave for two whole days. However, in spite of all the trees down, not one car nor any of the buildings were touched — and both were right in amongst the trees. Trees fell within inches of structures and autos but miraculously damaged nothing. For my friends, it was a great confirmation of their faith and willingness to trust.

Looking at this from a cause and effect standpoint, Jean recognized that buying insurance reinforced a belief (a cause) in adversity and would create the energy for something bad (an effect) to happen. Instead she chose the thought (cause) "We are doing God's work here, and we are totally safe." The effect, as it played out in the world, was that in the midst of chaos nothing bad happened.

As I have said, if you want to know your beliefs, look at what you have in your life — or what you do not have in your life. If, for example, you do not have love in your life and do not seem to be able to create a loving relationship, examine your beliefs about self-worthiness, or about safety with the opposite sex. Of course, this may not be as easy as it sounds, for the beliefs you hold may be buried deep in your subconscious mind.

You Don't Need To Know Why

The good news is that you do not have to know why you created your situation or what beliefs led to its creation. Just seeing the situation's existence as an opportunity to perceive it differently — *being willing* to see it as perfect — is enough to bring about the required shift in perception and a healing of the original pain.

The truth is, from the World of Humanity we cannot know *why* a situation is as it is, because the answer lies in the world of Divine Truth; and we can know little to nothing of that world as long as we are in human form. *All we can do is surrender to the situation.*

Just Surrender

If new insights, connections, old memories, emotional movements, and other psychic events are necessary for the desired change to occur, they will happen automatically and without our conscious control. If we try to figure it all out and manipulate the unfolding process, this creates resistance and blocks the process completely, which puts us right back under the influence of the Ego.

Freedom From the Law

It is therefore important to realize that the Law of Cause and Effect only applies to the World of Humanity. It is a physical law, not a spiritual law. Creating a parking space or any other physical thing that you desire and create with your mind is still only manipulating the illusion. It has little to do with being spiritual as such. In fact, if we imagine that we are special because of how well we can manifest in the world, this simply increases our sense of separation and strengthens the Ego.

On the other hand, when we truly drop the need to know the why or how of everything, let go of our need to control the world and truly surrender to what is — as is, in the knowledge that the love of God is in everything, we shall transcend the Law of Cause and Effect entirely. Then we shall realize that karma is just another story that exists only in our minds in the World of Humanity. In the World of Divine Truth, there is no such thing as Karma or Cause and Effect. There is only first cause which is God.

However, if we engage in activities and consistent ways of being that result in our vibration being significantly raised (*through the continual and sustained use of Radical Forgiveness over a long period of time for instance*), we may find ourselves becoming 'first cause.'

That would be in stark contrast to how it is for the majority of us at the present time, where we are always the 'effect' in this cause-and-effect world — always having to react to what appears to be happening 'out there.'

Perhaps, in the not-too-distant future, when our vibratory rate is raised and we have all our energy and consciousness in present time rather than tied up in past or future, we will find ourselves not so much 'noticing' synchronicities as 'becoming' synchronicity itself.

For more on how to gauge your own vibratory rate, how you stack up against the 'enlightened' ones and how many it would take of a certain vibration to shift planetary consciousness, I recommend David Hawkins's book, "Power vs. Force," published by Hay House.

9: Time, Medicine & Healing

Spiritual evolution brings with it a new appreciation for and knowledge of our physical bodies and how to care for them. The medical paradigm we have held for the last 300 years — ever since the French philosopher, Rene Descartes defined the body as a machine — is changing radically as it moves towards a holistic, mind-body approach.

We used to think of health as the absence of disease. Now, we think of health in terms of how well our *life-force* (prana, chi, etc), flows through our bodies. For optimum health this life-force must be able to flow freely. We cannot be healthy if our bodies are clogged with the energy of resentment, anger, sadness, guilt, and grief.

When we speak here of the body, we include not only the physical body, which is also an *energy body*, but the subtle bodies which surround us as well. These we refer to individually as the etheric body, the emotional body, the mental body, and the causal body. They each have a different frequency. Whereas we used to define the physical body in terms of chemicals and molecules, physicists have taught us to see all five bodies, including the physical body, as *dense condensations of interacting energy patterns.*

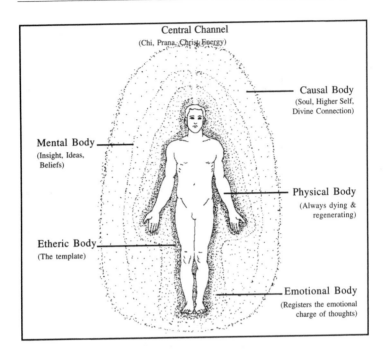

Fig. 8: The Subtle Energy Bodies

The subtle fields envelop the physical body in layers like vibrating sheaths of energy, each one an octave higher than the other. However, they are not fixed bands with clear boundaries as shown in the diagram above. Rather, they are, to a large degree, diffused within the same space as if they were all part of an ocean of energy surrounding our bodies. The subtle bodies are not so much defined by their position in space as by the different frequencies at which they vibrate.

The subtle bodies resonate harmonically with the vibrating patterns of the physical body, enabling consciousness (mind) to interact with the body. This is what we mean when we speak of the *body-mind continuum,* with mind existing both inside and outside the physical body. (For more details on the qualities and purpose ascribed to each of these subtle bodies, refer to Part 3, Chapter 15)

Clogged Filters Stress the Furnace

To ground this concept in a practical analogy, think of our bodies as being like the filters typically found in home heating furnaces — the kind we have to clean from time to time to ensure the furnace works efficiently. Just as these filters were designed to allow air to move easily through them, the same is true of our bodies. Life-force must be free to flow easily through all our bodies — our physical body and our subtle bodies, too.

Whenever we judge, make someone wrong, blame, project, repress anger, hold resentment, etc., we create an energy block in our body/bodies. Each time we do this, our filter becomes a little more blocked and less energy remains available for our *furnace.* Sooner or later the filter fails, and starved of the vital oxygen it must have to keep burning, the *flame* dies. More simply, when our physical and subtle bodies become too clogged for life-force to flow through easily, our body starts shutting down. In many cases, this manifests first as depression. Eventually, our body gets sick, and, if the blocks are not removed, we may die.

You may recall how my sister Jill felt a release of energy when she moved into Radical Forgiveness. Her life-force

93

filter was blocked by her toxic belief system about her own lack of worthiness, not to mention past resentments, anger, sadness, and frustrations over her current situation. When she let all that go, her energy blocks were cleared, which allowed her to shift her emotional state as well. Whenever you *forgive radically*, you release enormous amounts of life-force energy that then can be made available for healing, creativity, and expressing your true purpose in life.

Farra's Flu Release

My good friend Farra Allen, co-founder of the Atlanta School of Massage and a mind-body counselor, took ill with a particularly virulent strain of flu that typically kept people in bed for 10 days or more. It hit him hard, but instead of giving all his power to the virus, he decided to do some inner work around it, work that might shift the energy pattern holding the virus in place. Using a process known as *active imagination*, which simply involves writing down thoughts as a *stream of consciousness*, he came upon a hitherto unconscious and unresolved emotional issue. He used Radical Forgiveness to clear the issue, and the flu disappeared almost immediately. He was working full-time and feeling great within two days of the onset of his illness. This was a powerful demonstration of the healing power of Radical Forgiveness.

Will Cancer Respond Too?

Suppose the illness had been cancer rather than the flu, and it was our belief that it started as a deeply-repressed emotion. Thinking the cure lay in releasing that energy block, our recommendation might have been that my friend get in touch with the repressed feelings, feel them fully and then let them go.

However, unlike Farra's flu attack, which probably moved from his subtle body into his physical body in just a few days, this energy pattern might have taken many years to move from the subtle body into the physical body and, in time, to manifest as a disease. The question that haunts us then becomes, *'How long will it take for the disease process to fully reverse itself using emotional release work alone?'* Conceivably, it could require the same number of years it took for the disease to manifest — not very practical if you have cancer or some other disease where time is of the essence — or so it might seem, anyway.

Time Is a Factor In Healing

We used to think of time as something fixed and linear until Einstein proved that time actually is relative and that consciousness becomes a factor in the equation. The more elevated our consciousness, the faster we evolve and the faster things happen with regard to change in any physical matter to which we give attention.

Think of consciousness as our vibratory rate. It would probably take far too long to reverse the disease process of cancer energetically if we possess a low vibratory rate. It automatically will be low if we are in fear, hold anger and resentment in our beingness, think of ourselves as a victim, and/or have our energy locked up in the past. For the majority of us, this represents our consciousness most of the time. Therefore, few of us could reverse a disease like cancer fast enough relying solely on releasing the emotional cause of the disease — that is, unless we found a way to raise our vibratory rate.

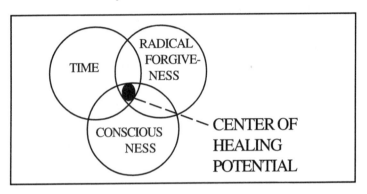

Fig. 9: Time & Healing.

By letting go of the victim archetype and bringing our energy into present time through the process of Radical Forgiveness, we might raise our vibration enough to create at least a quicker, if not immediate, disease reversal. We improve our chances if we also incorporate other ways of raising our vibration, such as prayer and meditation.

Example: A lady who attended one of our retreats had had several surgeries for ovarian cancer and had just been given by her doctors, at most, three months to live. She was depressed and had little life-force left. She said she only really came to the retreat because the people in her church had collected the money for her to come, so she felt obliged to do so. We worked with her and on the third day had a wonderful breakthrough that put her in touch with an event that had occurred when she was 2-1/2 years old and had made her believe herself to be utterly worthless. She released a lot of emotion around that issue and grieved for the countless number of times she had created her life in ways that proved her worthless. After that, her life-force energy increased. By the time she left she was all fired up to find an alternative program that would help her beat the cancer and the doctor's prognosis. She was even willing to travel outside the USA if the method she chose was illegal in this country. (Many are illegal in the USA.) After two weeks of frantically searching for the treatment to which she felt most drawn, she suddenly realized that her healing would come through prayer. So, she went away to a place in upstate New York and worked with a couple who offered prayer-weeks. She literally prayed for a week. Upon her return, she went to her oncologist who examined her and said, "I don't know how to explain this, but you have absolutely no cancer in your body. I could say it was a spontaneous remission, but I believe in God and I am not willing to describe it in any other way than as a miracle."

This woman serves as a wonderful example of how raising the vibration through prayer reversed the physical condition in days rather than years. I believe that Radical Forgiveness would have done the same.

Seattle Forgiveness Study

An interesting, but as yet unpublished, study on forgiveness and time was conducted at Seattle University. The study involved a series of interviews with people who, by their own assessment, had been victimized. The researchers wanted to see how that perception changed over time. Preliminary findings showed that serenity, which was described as "having no resentment left," came NOT through any act of forgiveness but as a sudden *discovery* that they had forgiven. All reported that the more they tried to forgive, the harder it became and the more resentment they felt. They stopped trying to forgive and *just let go.* After varying intervals of time came the surprising realization that they no longer harbored resentment and that they had, in fact, forgiven.

A later, and even more interesting, discovery revealed that the realization that they had forgiven was preceded by being forgiven themselves. (Who forgave them and for what was irrelevant.) However, what this certainly points to is that forgiveness is a shift in energy. Having experienced being forgiven — a release of stuck energy — they were able to release their own stuck energy with someone else.

This study not only reinforces the insight that forgiveness cannot be willed but also shows that forgiveness happens as an internal transformation through a combination of surrendering one's attachment to resentment and accepting forgiveness for oneself.

Additionally, this study's results underscore the value of Step Nine in the Twelve-Step process used successfully by millions of people in Alcoholics Anonymous and other similar programs. Step Nine asks that we seek to make amends with those we have harmed and that we ask those people for forgiveness. When we find that we have in fact been forgiven, this frees our own energy to forgive not only others but ourselves as well.

Time Heals - Fast or Slow

Some might argue that the Seattle study illustrates the slowness of the forgiveness process and shows that forgiveness would offer a rather ineffective method for curing a disease such as cancer. In many cases, it took people decades to discover they had forgiven.

The important distinction to make, however, is that the study did not distinguish between Radical Forgiveness and traditional forgiveness. What it described was definitely the latter. I would be willing to wager that, if the subject group had been divided into two — one group with insight into Radical Forgiveness and the other left basically to use traditional forgiveness, the group with the additional insight would have reached the serenity state infinitely more quickly than the other group.

I am not claiming that Radical Forgiveness always occurs instantaneously either — though I have to say I have seen it happen instantaneously many times now. Neither can it be claimed as a definitive *cure* for cancer. However, it certainly should be an integral part of any treatment protocol. Sometimes people delay medical treatment to see if Radical Forgiveness creates enough of an effect to make such drastic intervention unnecessary. That would be unthinkable with traditional forgiveness.

99

Mary's Story

My friend Mary Pratt, a co-facilitator at many of my retreats, denied for months that something was terribly wrong with her health. When she could not ignore the obvious any longer, she went to a doctor who told her she had stage three colon cancer. They wanted to operate immediately. She asked them for 30 days, and they reluctantly agreed. She went to a little cabin in the mountains and stayed there for a week, meditating and working on forgiving all the people in her life, including herself, using Radical Forgiveness. She fasted, prayed, cried, and literally went through *the dark night of the soul*. She came back home and worked with several practitioners to cleanse her body and strengthen her immune system.

At the end of the 30-day period, the surgery was performed. Afterwards, the doctor wanted to know what she had done, for the cancer had all but disappeared and instead of the radical surgery they had said would be necessary, removal of the cancer required only minor intervention.

Buying Time

In cases where the disease is so advanced or aggressive as to require immediate medical intervention, surgery, chemotherapy or radiation buys time. In that sense, such treatment becomes not only helpful but, at times, necessary.

Remember, there is no cure for cancer. Consequently, no matter what the medical treatment, the doctors have an unspoken expectation that a recurrence is almost a for-gone conclusion and just a question of time. I prefer to look at the treatment, assuming the patient survives it, as a way to buy the time to do the Radical Forgiveness work that could actually prevent any recurrence.

Preventive Medicine

Radical Forgiveness provides one of the best preventive measures available. Radical Forgiveness clears the energy in the subtle bodies long before it becomes a block in the physical body. When I help people resolve forgiveness issues by using Radical Forgiveness Therapy, like I did with my sister Jill, I believe I am not only helping them heal a wound in their subtle body, I am helping them prevent disease occurring in the physical body. I am convinced that if we keep the energy flowing in our bodies as it was designed to do, we never will get sick. Though I no longer do the five-day cancer retreats, I nevertheless regard the Radical Forgiveness workshops that I now present all around the world as cancer prevention workshops.

Of course, adequate exercise, good diet, and other such common sense practices help in this regard as well. However, keeping our energy bodies clear of emotional dross and toxicity is of primary importance to good health and healing. Unfortunately, this aspect of healing gets the least media attention, despite the fact that, in America alone, one out of every five people takes an antidepressant drug like Prozac. Bearing in mind that depression always precedes cancer, we have to wonder whether it is mere coincidence that one out of five Americans also dies of cancer.

Forgiveness and Cancer

I am often asked why I work with people who have cancer. I have had no personal experience with it, and I knew little about it from a medical standpoint when I began offering five-day cancer retreats for emotional and spiritual healing in the early 1990's.

It was only after doing this for some time that I realized why I was attracted to this work. It was because it linked up with my interest with forgiveness. That insight occurred when I discovered that nearly all cancer patients, besides having a lifetime habit of suppressing and repressing emotions, are known to share a marked inability to forgive.

I now believe that lack of forgiveness contributes to, and may even be a principal cause of, most cancers. Therefore, my healing work with cancer patients, and with those who want to prevent the disease from arising or reoccurring in their bodies, now centers almost entirely on Radical Forgiveness Therapy.

Jane's Story

Jane came to one of our five-day retreats in the North Georgia mountains. She had had a mastectomy and was awaiting a bone-marrow transplant. After the retreat, she came to me once a week for hypnotherapy and individual coaching. On the second visit she arrived in a distressed state, because a routine Magnetic Resonance Imaging (MRI) scan had that day discovered minute spots of cancer in her brain. While this new cancer was upsetting enough by itself, its appearance also was liable to spoil her chances of a transplant. The doctors planned to give her chemotherapy to try and arrest the cancer's progress. However, they were surprised at her condition, because normally metastasis proceeds from the breast to the liver and then to the brain. Very rarely does cancer proceed directly from the breast to the brain. To me, this seemed worthy of some exploration.

Jane, an attractive woman in her early forties, had not been involved in a romantic relationship for about seven years. She had a boyfriend of sorts, but she described the relationship as not much more than a close friendship. In fact, she said she looked upon him as her *buddy,* even though she had sex with him from time to time. As I probed further into her relationship situation, she got in touch with some incredible grief she still felt around a relationship she had ended a number of years ago. This eight-year relationship was extremely passionate and intense, and Jane clearly worshipped the man. Four years into this relationship, which she believed was soon to be consummated in marriage, she discovered that he was married already and had children. He had no intention of leaving his wife. Jane was devastated but could not stop seeing him. It took her another four extremely painful years to extricate herself from this relationship.

It was clear to me, that as a result of this failed relationship, Jane had shut down her emotions completely and would no longer allow herself to get involved so deeply with a man. Neither was I surprised that she had suffered a broken heart; most women with breast cancer have a broken heart somewhere in their history. (The breast is the organ of nurturance and is in the proximity of, and related to the heart.)

As she was going out the door at the end of our session, Jane said in a whisper, "I put him in the attic."

I stopped in my tracks. "What do you mean?" I asked.

"Well, everything I had accumulated over the years that had any connection to this man, or that would remind me of him, I stuffed in a box. I then put the box up in the attic. It's still there. I haven't touched it since."

I told her to sit down and tell me that again. I had her repeat the same thing three times. Suddenly, she saw the connection between the box in the attic that represented her broken love affair and her brain cancer. "Oh, my God," she said. "That's him in my head, isn't it? He's in my attic."

I told her to go home, go up into the attic and take down the box. I told her to bring it with her to her next session, and we would go through it piece by piece. We planned for her to tell me the story around each item until we had exorcised his energy and released the pain that she had repressed. Jane understood that this might be the key to her healing and was very excited. Tragically, she had a seizure the next day and was taken back to the hospital. She died a month later without ever touching the box in the attic. Looking at the box's contents and feeling the pain of her lost love may have been just too much for her to bear, and I feel, at some level, she may have decided to let go of life rather than face the pain.

Origins of Illness

Energy blocks always begin in the subtle bodies first. Then, if they are not released at that level, they move into the physical body and ultimately manifest as diseases such as cancer, multiple sclerosis, diabetes, and the like. Thus, we can say that illness always begins in the subtle bodies first and moves inward.

We used to think that the best way to stay ahead of disease was to visit a medical doctor for a regular checkup. We now know that we are much better off having a consultation with someone who can read our aura — meaning that they can tune into the energy patterns of our subtle bodies, particularly the etheric body. They can see blocks building energetically long before they show up in the physical body. Medical intuitives can do the same.

There are now also sophisticated technological diagnostic systems that do this. Called Electro-Dermal Screening Devices, they are mostly used by naturopaths, homeopaths, osteopaths and chiropractors. The machine uses the acupuncture points (which are in the etheric body), to get readings on each organ system of the body and to register disease at the subclinical level. These are proving to be very accurate devices, though as yet, most medical doctors fail to recognize them. Healing a disease pattern in the subtle body proves much easier than waiting for it to condense into physical matter, because once it does that, it becomes much more resistant to change.

Emotional Garbage

Quantum physicists have actually proven that emotions condense as energy particles, which, if not expressed as emotion, become lodged in the spaces between atoms and molecules. That literally is the filter becoming clogged. Once the emotion has become a particle, it becomes much more difficult to release, and therein lies the problem. It takes much more time and effort to release that block from the physical body than it would have if it had been released while still in pure energy form in the subtle body/bodies — in this case the emotional body. However, shifting those particles before they do harm is possible, and the best way I know to do so is through Radical Forgiveness.

Why We Don't Heal

Clearly, time and healing are directly related. For us to evolve to the extent that we can heal ourselves, we must have most of our consciousness in present time — not in the past, not in the future, but in the *now*. Caroline Myss, in her tape series, *Why People Don't Heal,* maintains that people with more than 60 percent of their life energy siphoned off to maintain the past are unable to heal themselves energetically. Thus, they remain totally reliant upon chemical medicine for their healing.

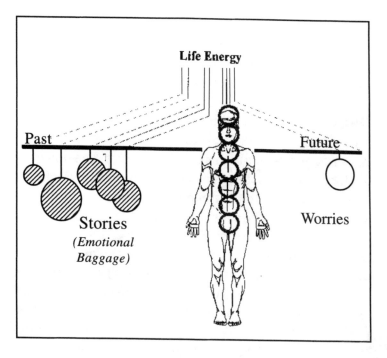

Fig. 10: Why People Don't Heal

She argues that if it takes 60 to 70 percent of the average person's precious life-force to manage the negative experiences of his or her childhood, adolescence and earlier years of adulthood, as well as to hold on to the losses, disappointments, and resentments of the past, and another 10 percent worrying about, planning for and trying to control the future, that leaves precious little energy for the present moment — or for healing. (It is important to note that it does not drain our energy to maintain positive memories nor even negative memories if they have been processed and forgiven.)

Life has its own way of bringing us — and our energy — into present time. Often it is through trauma. When we find ourselves in the midst of a disaster, have an unexpected accident, or discover that our lives suddenly are in danger, we become very focused on the present moment. We bring all our consciousness into the present instinctively. Suddenly, the past does not matter. The future does not matter. Only this moment exists. The power of such currently-focused energy is demonstrated when a mother, seeing her child trapped under a car, suddenly becomes able to lift the car off the ground so her child can be rescued. Acts of incredible bravery and courage also happen when energy becomes focused in the moment, because fear only occurs when we bring the past into the future. When we are truly in the moment we are absolutely fearless, because we have no awareness of past or future.

Radical Forgiveness helps us be in present time, because we do not *forgive radically* by going back into the past. We simply forgive the person who happens to be mirroring our projection right here in the present. That is the beauty of Radical Forgiveness. It is true that sometimes the past connection will be so clear, as in Jill's case, it illuminates the current situation. However, the focus is still on the perfection of what is happening *in the now*. We can either choose to let go of the victim archetype and bring our energy into the present through Radical Forgiveness or wait for a significant trauma to force us into the now. In other words, we can either transform our consciousness as a matter of will, or we can wait for a disaster or a life-threatening illness to make us do it.

PART THREE

Tools for
Radical Forgiveness

10: A Spiritual Technology

In writing the first edition of this book I had two objectives in mind. First, I wanted to explain the concept of Radical Forgiveness as simply as I could to make it accessible to as many people as possible. Second, I wanted to make it as practical as I could so that people could use it in their everyday lives. That meant having tools that were not only effective but quick and easy to use.

As I write this second edition, I confess that the extent to which the tools in this book have proven effective more than surprises me. I find myself in awe of how extraordinarily powerful they have proven to be in helping people heal their lives.

I have also come to realize that they work in a way not dissimilar to how homeopathic remedies work. That is to say they work holo-energetically *(using the energy of the whole)*.

Being part of a holographic universe, each minute part of the universe is not only connected energetically to the whole, but contains the whole. Therefore, from an energetic standpoint, you cannot change one part of it without it affecting the whole.

Homeopathy uses this principle by making remedies that affect the energy system of the organism in exactly this way. The tiniest part of an active ingredient is put into water and it is then diluted many thousands of times to the point where there is no physical trace of the substance left. What does remain however, is the energetic imprint of the substance and therein lies the power to heal. When the person takes the remedy, the subtle body registers the imprint and becomes stimulated to move energy in whatever way it needs in order to heal at all levels.

The same thing happens with these Radical Forgiveness tools. Just as someone might look at the homeopathic remedy and would, seeing only water, find great difficulty in imagining that it has the power to heal, so might someone looking at a forgiveness worksheet, for example, be totally sceptical about its ability to change her life.

Yet it works. Thousands of people have used the worksheet or listened to the 13 Steps CD or walked the circle in the Radical Forgiveness Ceremony and have experienced miracles in their lives.

These tools work because each of them is simply the delivery system for the secret ingredient — the energetic imprint of Radical Forgiveness; i.e. the *willingness* to be open to the idea that there is nothing to forgive.

The process is very subtle. Mind control or making things happen at the gross level through affirmations, visualization techniques or hypnosis has little relevance to Radical Forgiveness. Neither does it require a high level of belief or faith; nor do you need to be in a meditative or altered state. All you need to do is use a simple tool that asks little of you in the way of intelligence, discipline or skill. It asks only that you express a tiny amount of willingness — that's all. In this second edition of the book, I have even simplified the worksheet so that in some places you only have to check boxes in answer to a few questions. It still works.

Since forgiveness is always a 'fake-it-'til you-make-it,' proposition, we are indeed fortunate that it needs only that small amount. If you had to wait until you had 100% willingness to believe that the situation was perfect, you would never begin the process.

The following story is an example of how this transformation can occur in an instant using one of the Radical Forgiveness tools - interestingly enough, the quickest and simplest of them all — the *13 Steps to Radical Forgiveness.*

Debi and the 13 Steps

Debi was a studio singer which means she sang jingles, commercials, radio ID's and things like that. She was considered to be among the best in the business. In 1999, she came to study with me to become a Radical Forgiveness Coach.

At one point during the training, I wanted to teach her how to facilitate the *13 Steps to Radical Forgiveness.* It takes no more than seven minutes and involves responding in the affirmative to thirteen very simple questions.

The thirteen questions all relate to one's willingness (the secret ingredient) to see the perfection in the situation whether

113

they understand it or not. The answer to each question is 'Yes.' I asked Debi if she had a situation to work with for this process. She thought for a while and then said: *"Yes, here's something I've been upset about for a while. I'd almost forgotten. About thirteen years ago, I was in a particular studio and in came a guy that I knew reasonably well, but was not real close to. We chatted for a while and eventually he came out with what was really on his mind. He said, "Debi, I have this great product that's just perfect to market on the radio and I need you to do an ad for me. The problem is, I don't have money right now, but will you do it as a big favor to me?"*

Well, I finally gave in and agreed to do for $75 what I normally charge a lot of money for. I did the ad, and what d'you know, it made him a multi-millionaire overnight.

Sometime later, when I ran into him, I suggested he might want to send just a little bit of that my way in appreciation of what I had done for him. His response was, "Debi, we're not in the business of giving money away!"

This was perfect. She was obviously into her feelings about it — even after thirteen years! This was understandable given the fact that every time she had turned the radio on over the last thirteen years, there would be that ad! As you might imagine it had all the ingredients of a victim story — betrayal, insult, manipulation, withholding, ingratitude, and so on.

So I immediately proceeded to take her through the process. It took no more than the seven minutes, and as always after doing a process like that, we went on to something else without any further discussion. (Talking about it would destroy the energy field created in the process).

She went out that evening and returned to her hotel at around 11:00 pm. She called me at 11:05 in a state of great excitement. Apparently she had checked her voice mail messages and one was from the studio producer who had helped her do that particular ad.

The message went like this: "Debi, that commercial you recorded for Mr. X. has come up again, and it needs to be re-recorded. However, the copyright has expired, so you could earn all the royalties on it this time. Are you interested?"

Well, as you might imagine, I was jumping up and down yelling, "Hey, this stuff really works!" But then Debi says, "But there's more. When we did the 13 steps," Debi went on, "I happened to glance at the clock on the wall, and for some reason I registered the time quite clearly in my mind. It was 3:01 pm. That message came in at 3:02 pm! One minute after — and I haven't spoken with him for months!"

Debi's victim story about how she was used, cheated, dishonored, insulted, and rejected had kept the energy stuck for thirteen years. It was not until she was invited to express a minute amount of willingness to see that she had created that story out of her own perception of the situation, and during the 13 Steps process, reframed it in a way that reflected spiritual truth, that the energy field collapsed. At no point did we "work" on her story. That would only have given it more power and reinforced it. Instead we used the holo-energetic

115

technology of Radical Forgiveness to transform the energy. It is interesting to look at what might have been happening here. Most people would have agreed with Debi that this man had betrayed, insulted and dishonored her by his selfish attitude. Yet the very fact that he exhibited this really quite peculiar kind of behavior was a clue that something else was going on beneath the apparent situation.

At the time that event occurred, Debi's self esteem was very low. Even though she was always being told how good a singer she was, she could never accept it. She would always put herself down. She had an unconscious belief that she wasn't worthy of what she could rightly charge for her talent.

It is a principle of Radical Forgiveness that if you have a limiting belief that prevents you from becoming whole or from achieving your true purpose, your Higher Self will always find a way to acquaint you with your limiting belief so you can heal it. It can't intervene directly because you have free will. But it can, through the Law of Attraction, bring into your life someone who will act out your belief for you so you might see it for what it is and choose to let it go.

This man resonated with her limiting belief that she was unworthy, not good enough, and undeserving and responded to the call. His Higher Self colluded with her Higher Self to play this worthiness issue out so she got to feel the pain of this idea in order that she might see it and choose again.

Far from being a villain then, this man was, in fact, a healing angel for Debi. At great discomfort to himself — for who

11: The Five Stages of RF

No matter the form that the technology of Radical Forgiveness takes, whether it be a workshop, the 13 Steps, the Radical Forgiveness worksheet or the ceremony, each is designed to take you through the five essential stages of Radical Forgiveness. These are:

1. Telling the Story:

In this step, someone willingly and compassionately listens to us tell our story and honors it as being our truth in the moment. (If we are doing a worksheet, this person might be ourself).

Having our story heard and witnessed is the first and vital step to letting it go. Just as the first step in releasing victimhood is to own it fully, so must we own our story in its fullness from the point of view of being a victim and avoid any spiritual interpretation at this stage. This comes later in step 4.

Here, we must begin from where we are (or were, if we are going back into the past to heal something), so that we can feel some of the pain that caused the energy block in the first place.

2. Feeling the Feelings:

This is the vital step that many so-called spiritual people want to leave out, thinking that they shouldn't have 'negative' feelings. That's denial, pure and simple, and misses the crucial point that authentic power resides in our capacity to feel our feelings fully and in that way show up as fully human. It is only when we give ourselves permission to access our pain that our healing begins. The healing journey is essentially an emotional journey. But it doesn't have to be all pain either. It is surprising as we go down through the levels of emotion and allow ourselves to feel the authentic pain, how quickly it can turn to peace, joy, and thankfulness.

3. Collapsing the Story:

This step looks at how our story began and how our interpretations of events led to certain (false) beliefs forming in our minds that have determined how we think about ourselves and how we have lived our lives. When we come to see that these stories are for the most part untrue and serve only to keep us stuck in the victim archetype, we become empowered to make the choice to stop giving them our vital life force energy. Once we decide to retrieve our energy, we take back our power and the stories wither and die.

It is also at this step that we might exercise a high degree of compassion for the person we are forgiving and bring to the table some straightforward honest to goodness understanding of how life often is, just how imperfect we all are, and the realization that we are all doing the very best we can with what we are given. Much of this we might categorize as traditional forgiveness, but it is nevertheless important as a first step and a reality check. After all, most of our stories have their genesis in early childhood when we imagined that the whole world revolved around us and that everything was our fault.

So this is where we can give up some of that child-centered woundedness merely by bringing our adult perspective to bear on it and confronting our own inner child with the plain truth of what really did or didn't happen as distinct from our interpretations about what we think happened. It is amazing how ridiculous many of our stories seem once we allow the light in. However, the real value in this step is in our releasing our attachment to the story, so we can more easily begin to make the transition required in the next step.

4. Reframing the Story:

This is where we allow ourselves to shift our perception in such a way that instead of seeing the situation as a tragedy, we become willing to see that it was in fact exactly what we wanted to experience and was absolutely essential to our growth. In that sense it was perfect. At times we will be able to see the perfection right away and learn the lesson immediately. Most often, however, it is a matter of giving up the need to figure it out and surrendering to the idea that the gift is contained in the situation whether we know it or not. It is in that act of surrender that the real lesson of love is learned and the gift received. This is also the step of transformation for as we begin to become open to seeing the Divine perfection in

121

what happened, our victim stories that were once the vehicles for anger, bitterness and resentment become transformed into stories of appreciation, gratitude and loving acceptance.

5. Integration:

After we have allowed ourselves to be willing to see the perfection in the situation and turned our stories into ones of gratitude, it is necessary to integrate that change at the cellular level. That means integrating it into the physical, mental, emotional and spiritual bodies so it becomes a part of who we are. It's like saving what you have done on the computer to the hard drive. Only then will it become permanent.

With the worksheet, the integration comes through the writing and reading the statements out loud. With the 13 Steps, it is making the verbal affirmation to see the perfection. With the ceremony it is in the act of walking across the circle and saying something of an affirmative nature to someone else coming in the other direction. Ritual, ceremony, and, of course, music is also used to integrate the shift in perception that is Radical Forgiveness.

These five stages don't necessarily occur in this order. Very often we move through them, or some of them at least, simultaneously, or we keep coming back and forth from one stage to another in a kind of circular or spiralling fashion.

12: Fake It 'Til You Make It

Forgiveness is a journey, and it always begins from a place of nonforgiveness. Getting there can take years or minutes, and we know now that this is a matter of choice. Traditional forgiveness takes a long time, but we can do it quickly through Radical Forgiveness simply by expressing our *willingness* to see the perfection. Each time we do this, it represents an act of faith, a prayer, an offering, a humble request for Divine assistance. We do this at moments when we feel unable to forgive, and in that sense it is a fake-it-'til-you-make it process.

Surrendering

Faking it until you make it really means surrendering to the process, putting forth no effort nor trying to control the results. In the Seattle study (Chapter 13), the more effort the participants put into trying to forgive, the more difficult they found it to let go of their hurt and anger. When they stopped trying to forgive and to control the process, at some point in time forgiveness just happened.

It is true that the energetic shift from anger and blame to forgiveness and responsibility happens much more quickly with Radical Forgiveness because, using the tools given here, we can drop the victim consciousness.

123

Consciousness, you will recall from Chapter 13, changes time. Nevertheless, even with Radical Forgiveness, we must enter the process with no expectation of when an energy shift might happen — even though we know that it can happen instantaneously. Exactly when the results begin to show up may depend on things we know little about. It might take a while before we begin to really feel unconditional acceptance for the person involved and peace around the situation — which is how we know when the forgiveness process is complete. It might take many worksheets, for example, to reach this point.

However, it will be of comfort to many to learn that we do not have to like the person to forgive them. Neither do we have to stay in their company if their personality and/or their behavior is toxic to us. Radical Forgiveness is a soul-to-soul interaction and requires only that we become connected at the soul level. When we feel this unconditional love for their soul, our soul joins theirs, and we become one.

Taking the Opportunity

Any time someone upsets us, we must recognize this as an opportunity to forgive. The person upsetting us may be resonating something in us that we need to heal, in which case he or she gives us a gift, if we choose to see it that way; that is, if we care to *shift our perception*. The situation also may be a replay of earlier times when someone did something similar to us. If so, this current person represents all the people who have ever done this to us before. As we forgive this person for the current situation, we forgive all others who behaved likewise, as well as forgiving ourselves for what we might have projected onto them.

An example of this appears as a diagram on page 36. Here, Jill's story is represented as a time-line on which appear all the opportunities she had been given to heal her original pain arising out of her misperception that she was "not enough." When she finally saw what was happening in the situation with Jeff and forgave him (healed), she automatically forgave and healed every previous occasion - including the original one with her father. Her entire story, including those connected to her previous husband, collapsed in an instant as soon as that light bulb went on.

This is why Radical Forgiveness requires no therapy as such. Not only does forgiving in the moment heal all the other times the same or similar thing happened, including the original situation, but you don't have to know what the original situation was. That means you don't have to go digging up the past trying to figure out exactly what the original pain was. It is healed anyway, so what's the point?

Shifting Our Perception

The following chapters contain processes that shift energy and offer opportunities to *change our perception* of what might be happening in a given situation. This change in perception constitutes the essence of Radical Forgiveness. All of these processes bring us into the present moment by helping us retrieve our energy from the past and withdraw it from the future, both of which must be done for change to occur. When we are in the present moment, we cannot feel resentment, because resentment only lives in the past. Neither can we feel fear, because fear only exists in relation to the future. We find ourselves, therefore, with the opportunity to be in present time and in the space of love, acceptance, and Radical Forgiveness.

First Aid Forgiveness Tools

Some of the Q-Work tools are more appropriate for use at the very moment when a situation requiring forgiveness occurs. They help jerk us into an awareness of what may be happening before we get drawn too deeply into a drama and go to victimland. When our *buttons get pushed,* we easily move straight into the defense/attack cycle. Once in this cycle, however, we find it tough to get out. Use of these quick tools, however, helps us avoid ever beginning the cycle. The Four-Steps to Forgiveness process is one of these. It is easy to remember and you can say it to yourself in the moment. The 13 Steps to Forgiveness or CD is also very useful because you can have that in the car or handy at home.

Other tools are designed for use in quiet solitude after we have had a chance to vent anger and frustration. These Q-Work programs work wonders in this regard. Use them as an act of faith in the beginning. The payoff will prove incredible in time. Consistent use of these tools helps us find a peace we may never have known was even possible.

13: Feeling the Pain

Feeling the feelings is the second stage in the forgiveness process and usually arises as a consequence of telling the story. This step requires that we give ourselves permission to feel the feelings we have around a given situation — and to feel them fully. If we try to forgive using a purely mental process, thus denying that we feel angry, sad, or depressed, for example, nothing happens. I have met many people, especially those who think of themselves as spiritual, who feel that feelings are to be denied and 'given-over' to Spirit. That's what is known as a spiritual bypass.

In 1994, I agreed to do a workshop in England. This was ten years after I had emigrated to America and I had quite forgotten the extent to which English people resist feeling their feelings.

The workshop was to take place in a monastery somewhere in the west of England, and as it happened, most of the participants were spiritual healers. We arrived at the monastery, but there was no one around, so we went in, rearranged the furniture, and began the workshop. I began by explaining that life was essentially an emotional experience for the purpose of our spiritual growth and that the workshop was designed to help us get in touch with emotions that we have buried.

Well, you would have thought I was telling them that they had to dance naked around a fire or something! Here's what they said.

"Oh, no. We are spiritual. We have transcended our emotions. We don't give our emotions any credence at all. If we have them, we simply ask Spirit to take them away, and we simply go straight to peace. We don't believe in this kind of work."

By about one hour into the workshop, I knew I had a disaster on my hands. It was like swimming through treacle. I couldn't get through at all, and there was no way they were going to do this work. I was feeling progressively more awful every moment and was convinced that the workshop was going to fall apart completely.

At this point Spirit intervened. A young monk in full habit burst into the room demanding to know who was in charge. When I said I was, he demanded that I go outside with him. He wanted to "talk" to me, but I could see that he was seething with anger. He was all red and puffed up. I said that I was conducting a seminar and that I would come and find him when I was finished.

He went out very upset but came back almost immediately, clearly enraged. He pointed his finger at me and then hooked it as if to motion me towards him, and screamed. "I want to see you, right now!"

It was the gesture with the finger that got me. All the frustration and tension of the last hour came rushing to the surface. I turned to my class and said in a very menacing tone. *"Just watch this!"* I strode over to the red-faced, puffed-up monk and told him in no uncertain terms, pointing back at him with my finger very close to his face, *"I don't care what you are wearing and what those clothes represent, you don't come into my workshop and hook me out as if I were some little schoolboy who has offended you. I'll come out and talk to you when — and only when — I am ready. In fact, I will be done right at 12:00 noon. If you have anything to say to me, you'd better be outside in the lobby right at that time. Then we can talk. Now, get out of my room!"*

I strode back to my class, all of whom were sitting there aghast with their mouths gaping. (You don't talk to religious figures like that!) *"Right,"* I said, pointing to each one of them in turn, *"I want to know what you are feeling right now, in this moment, and don't give me that B.S. that you have given it to the violet flame and that you are feeling peaceful, because it is obvious that you are not. What are you feeling?!!! Get real!!"*

Well, needless to say they were in their feelings big time, and we started to discuss them. With the help of the monk, I had broken through their wall of resistance to acknowledging that humans have feelings and that they are OK. I had busted their story. They were doing the spiritual bypass and I let them know it.

At 12:00 noon, I went out of the room into the lobby. The monk was there. I went straight up to him, and much to his surprise and consternation, I hugged him. *"Thank you so*

129

much," I said, *"You were a healing angel for me today. You were my seminar. You saved the whole thing."*

He really didn't know what to say. I don't think he got it either, even when I tried to explain it to him. He had calmed down though, and it turned out that all he was so upset about was that I had not rung the bell to let him know that we were there. He had been sitting in his room waiting for the bell to ring, not thinking that we might push open the door and go on in. Can you imagine getting so enraged about such a small thing? Do you think he might have had an abandonment or "not-good-enough" issue running?

That 7-day retreat became one of the best workshops I have ever done. That's because the participants got real and became authentic. I took them into their pain, some of which dated back to war-time incidences they had never shared before. They came to realize that the power to heal is in the feelings, not in talking or thinking; not in affirmations, nor even in meditation if it includes shutting out feelings.

Another myth is that there are two kinds of feeling, positive and negative, and that negative ones must be avoided. The truth is there is no such thing as a negative emotion. They only become *bad* and have a negative effect on us when they are suppressed, denied, or unexpressed. Positive thinking is really just another form of denial.

We Want the Emotional Experience

As human beings, we are blessed with the capability to feel our emotions. In fact, some say the *only* reason we have chosen this human experience arises from the fact that this is the only planet carrying the vibration of emotional energy, and we have come here precisely to experience it. Consequently, when we do not allow ourselves to experience the full range of emotions and suppress them instead, our souls create situations in which we literally are forced to feel them. (Haven't you noticed that people often are given opportunities to feel intense emotions just after having prayed for spiritual growth?)

This means that the whole point of creating an upset may simply lie in our soul's desire to provide an opportunity for us to feel a suppressed emotion. That being the case, simply allowing ourselves to have the feeling might allow the energy to move through us and the so-called problem to disappear immediately.

However, not all situations are dissolved that easily. When we try coping with a deep-seated issue and a remembrance of what seems an unforgivable transgression, such as sexual abuse, rape, or physical abuse, it takes more than just experiencing our emotions to get to the point where we feel unconditional love for that person. Feeling the emotion fully is just the first step in faking it until we make it and definitely cannot be bypassed.

I am not saying that the emotional work will not benefit from insight gained through a shift in perception that might have occurred before the emotions were felt and expressed. It certainly will. However, the converse does not hold true; the perceptual shift required for Radical Forgiveness will

131

not happen if the underlying repressed feelings are not released first.

Invariably, when we feel the desire to forgive someone or something, we have at some time felt anger toward them or it. Anger actually exists as a secondary emotion. Beneath anger lies a primary emotional pain, such as hurt pride, shame, frustration, sadness, terror, or fear. Anger represents *energy in motion* emanating from the suppression of that pain. Not allowing one's anger to flow can be likened to trying to cap a volcano. One day it will blow!

Stages one and two in the Radical Forgiveness process ask us to get in touch with not only the anger but the underlying emotion as well. This means feeling it — not talking about it, analyzing it, or labeling it, but experiencing it!

Love Your Anger

All too often when people talk about *letting go* of anger or *releasing* anger, they really mean trying to get rid of it. They judge it as wrong and undesirable — even frightening. They do not want to feel it, so they just talk about it and try to process it intellectually, but that does not work. Trying to process emotion through talking about it is just another way to resist feeling it. That's why most talk therapies don't work. **What you resist persists**. Since anger represents energy in motion, resisting it just keeps it stuck within us — until the volcano erupts. Releasing anger actually means freeing the stuck energy of held emotions by allowing them to move freely through the body as feeling.

Doing some kind of *anger work* helps us experience this emotion purposefully and with control.

Anger Work Moves Energy

What we call anger work is not really about anger. It is simply the process of getting energy stuck in the body moving again. It might be more appropriately called energy release work. Whatever we call it, the process can be as simple as screaming into a cushion (so as not to alarm neighbors), yelling in the car, beating cushions, chopping wood, or doing some other explosive physical activity.

Combining physical activity with the use of the voice seems to provide the key to successful energy release work. All too often we block the energy of emotion in the throat, whether that be anger, sadness, guilt, or whatever else, so vocal expression should always be a part of the process. We should go into it, not with the idea of trying to rid ourselves of the feeling, but with the intention of feeling the intensity of it moving through our body — without thought or judgment. If we truly can surrender to the emotions, we will feel more alive than we have felt in a long while, and we will find that the energy has dissipated.

If Anger Is Scary

For many of us, the thought of bringing up anger may be too scary even to contemplate, especially if terror lies underneath the anger. The person who did these terrible things to us may still exert a strong influence on our subconscious mind. Under these circumstances, it would not be advisable to do anger work alone. Instead, we should work with someone who knows how to support us while we feel both the anger and the terror — someone with whom we feel safe and who has experience in helping people move through intense emotion. A counselor or psychotherapist of some kind would be a good choice. I also recommend doing Satori Breathwork (see Chapter 27) with a skilled practitioner. This provides a way to release emotion.

Anger Addiction Warning

A note of caution needs to be sounded here. It becomes all too easy to get addicted to anger. Anger feeds on itself and easily becomes resentment. Resentment relishes going over and over an old hurt, constantly revisiting the pain associated with it and venting the resultant anger in some form. It becomes a powerful addiction in and of itself.

We must realize that anger that persists serves no useful purpose. Consequently, once the energy of anger has been allowed to flow as feeling, we should use the energy to create a positive outcome. Maybe we need to set a boundary or a condition on future interactions with the person around whom our anger revolves. Perhaps we can make a decision of some kind, such as to be willing to feel compassion for the person or to forgive the person. Only when used as the catalyst for positive change, self-empowerment or forgiveness will we prevent the anger from becoming an addictive cycle.

14: Collapsing the Story

The story is where the pain resides. It is what we write in Box #1 of the worksheet to complete the sentence *'The situation as I see it now is....'*

Since it appears to be the source of all our pain and discomfort, it is worth turning the spotlight on our victim story to see the extent to which it is real and whether holding on to the pain is justified. We might find that there's very little in it that is actually true. We might find that it is just a story we have created to keep us stuck in separation in order to reinforce our belief that we are not all One. It might also be that we have created this story to give us clues as to what we might be needing to heal (forgive) within ourselves so that we can come to the realization that we are indeed all One.

Obviously it is this last possibility to which Radical Forgiveness gives attention, for it is our belief that the very purpose of the story — and of course the role of all the players within it — is to highlight and bring to conscious awareness that which needs healing. It is in the dismantling of the story that we find our opportunity to learn the real truth about ourselves and to remember who we really are.

In the process of tracing back how the story got formed we can usually see how a false negative core belief was first created, then repressed, and subsequently made active in the subconscious mind such that it would continue to create circumstances to reinforce itself. This is what happened to Jill. (see Chapter One). Her unconscious core belief was, "I'm not good enough for any man," and she lived it out. Once we collapsed the story and she saw that it was not true, she healed the core belief and everything worked out.

These core beliefs usually form when we are very young. When something happens to us, we interpret that experience and give personal meaning to the situation. Then, we confuse what really happened with our interpretation of what happened. The story we *make up* based on that mixture of fact and fiction becomes our truth and an operating principle in our lives.

For example, let's say our father leaves home when we are five years old. For us, this event is traumatic and painful, but in our mind that is only the beginning of our story. At that age we think the world revolves around us so we can only see it from that egocentric point of view. So we make our own interpretations based on that viewpoint. Our first interpretation is that *he left ME!* After that come many more that expand the story egocentrically, such as: *"It must be my fault. I must have done something to drive him away. He doesn't love me any more. Maybe he never did. I must be a very unlovable person if my father would leave me. He can't care about me and if he doesn't care about me, who will?*

I guess if he doesn't love me nobody will love me, and even if they do they are sure to leave me after five years because that's the way things are with men who say they love you. You can't really trust men who say they love you because they are bound to leave after 5 years anyway. I am just not very lovable. I will never have a relationship that will last more than five years. If I was not good enough for my father, I will never be good enough for anyone."

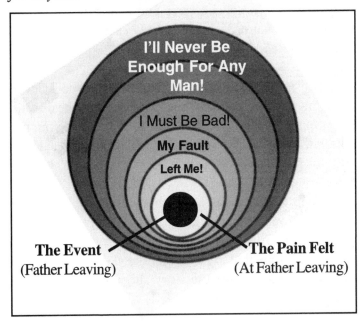

Fig. 11: How A (False) Story Grows

We might also, if we are female, as happened with someone in my workshop recently who had this story running, make it up that men are always subject to being 'stolen' by other women and unconsciously create situations where this happens — in this example after about five years of being in relationship.

These stories become like internal gyroscopes with their own frequencies that attract events and people to them so they get played out according to the beliefs they contain. But as we can see, the only part of the story that is true is the original event. Father left. That might be perhaps 5% of the total story. The rest is simply interpretation — assumptions made by a very immature, frightened mind. That makes the story 95% B.S! *(Belief System)?*

Your Higher Self knows that those ideas are not only B.S. but highly toxic as well, so while it cannot intervene directly since Spirit gave us free will, it brings people into your life who will lovingly "act out" parts of your story over and over until you realize that it is not true.

Again, this is what happened with my sister Jill. When our father demonstrated the kind of love for my daughter, Lorraine, that Jill always wanted to feel from him and had not felt, Jill took that to mean that she was inherently unlovable. That became the story she believed until she brought someone into her life (Jeff) who was able to make her discover her story and to see that it was false.

Discovering the story is half the battle. Sometimes you are aware of it, sometimes not. Glenda was a sophisticated, intelligent, attractive, and accomplished woman in her late forties. She had never been married. In fact, she had never had a relationship that lasted more than two or three years. It seemed she could never meet *Mr. Right.* Whenever she got to know a man well, she discovered something about him that annoyed her or made her feel dissatisfied with the relationship. So she would end the relationship. This happened over and over again. She did not see it as a problem, though. As a career woman, she said her job provided her with a lot of satisfaction. On the other hand, she did concede that she was lonely.

One day a good friend asked her, "Have you ever wondered why you don't hold onto a relationship? Have you ever thought that maybe it's not the *something* that you see in them that makes you annoyed or dissatisfied but the *something* in you that you haven't dealt with that won't let you have a decent relationship with a man?"

At the time Glenda just shrugged off her friend's words, but later she began thinking more deeply about her friend's query. She decided to work with a therapist to see if anything lay behind her relationship pattern. The therapist hypnotized her and then regressed her to the age of eight.

Under hypnosis, she recalled that, at that age, she would come home from school every day to play with her best friend, Mark. They had been close friends since they were very young and were truly inseparable at this point in time. Then she recalled an incident that happened one day after she had changed out of her school clothes and run over to Mark's house. She knocked on the door, and no one answered. She put her face close to the glass and peered

139

in. Her heart sank when she saw the house was empty. Where was everyone? Where was the furniture? Where was Mark? She did not understand — not until she turned to leave the front porch and saw a small sign lying flat in the grass. It said, 'SOLD.'

It slowly dawned on Glenda that Mark's parents had sold the house and gone away taking Mark with them — gone without saying a word, without so much as a good-bye, without even telling her. Mark had never even mentioned that he was moving.

Hurt and confused, Glenda sat on the porch for a few hours before walking the short distance home. She remembered making two decisions during that time. The first was to say nothing to her parents. If they mentioned Mark being gone, she would pretend she did not care. The second decision was never to trust a boy (man) again.

She had apparently forgotten all about this incident, but when it surfaced during her therapy session she became upset. The years of repressed grief over being abandoned by her best friend poured out as did the rage over what she saw as a betrayal.

After the session, she went to see her mother. She talked about Mark and asked her mother what happened to him and his family. "Oh, his father got transferred," her mother said. "It all happened quite quickly, but we were very surprised that you said nothing about their leaving. We thought you'd be really upset, but you seemed to just take it in your stride. In fact we and Mark's parents talked before they left because all of us were concerned that you and Mark would be terribly upset. We all agreed it would be best in the long run if we didn't tell either of you anything about the move until the day it actually happened. They didn't even put a 'For Sale' sign up on the house. It was not until Mark was in the car and on the way to their new home that they even told him."

Glenda was stunned. If Mark did not know about the move, then he had not betrayed her after all. At that moment the realization hit her — for more than 30 years she had allowed a completely buried subconscious story to rule her life and to spoil every romantic relationship she had ever had. Not only that, the idea itself was based on a totally false assumption.

As soon as any man got close enough to Glenda to be her friend and her lover, she ended the relationship. She believed that if she got close to a man, like she had been with Mark, he would abandon and betray her in the same way. She was not going to risk suffering that degree of pain again, not for any man. Not only that, she shut down, or suppressed, her feelings of abandonment and betrayal on the day she discovered Mark had moved. Later, she poured herself into her career as a way of avoiding those feelings.

The friend who confronted Glenda with her self-defeating pattern saw beyond her *story* and recognized that something else was going on. She had created many healing opportunities but had missed them all.

141

Glenda came to a Radical Forgiveness workshop and forgave the man with whom she had separated most recently and, as a consequence, all the others that she had judged as 'not trustworthy' before him. That automatically neutralized the original idea that she could never trust a man again so she became free to have the relationship that she really wanted.

Unlike Glenda, Jesse, another workshop participant, appeared fully aware of her story but still did not see the mistake in it. This was in spite of the fact that she was spiritually very aware. She was at one of my workshops and told us that she had just been fired from her job. "That's OK," she said, "It's my abandonment issue playing itself out again. I get fired or lose a relationship every couple of years. It's because I was abandoned when I was a baby."

I suspected a B.S. story so I began to investigate the abandonment. What we soon discovered was that her father had died just before she was born and that her mother had become ill and unable to cope when Jesse was about two years old . Consequently, Jesse was reared for a while by her grandparents.

Though she was no doubt traumatized by being separated from her mother, the actual truth of the matter was that her parents never did abandon her. They were simply absent through no fault of their own. They certainly did not abandon her. To abandon someone is to make a calculated and conscious choice to leave them. It is a deliberate act. Mere absence does not constitute abandonment.

Taking absence to mean abandonment was an interpretation that a small child might easily make and yet the importance goes way beyond semantics. Interpreting her parents' absence as abandonment, she went on to make a number of other interpretations such as: *"If my parents abandon me, then I must be a very unlovable person. No one will ever stay with me for more than 2 years because, if my mother abandons me after that time, everyone will do exactly that. They won't want me after that. They will realize that I am a bad person and will leave. That's how life is."*

Jesse had been living out of this particular story for all her 52 years. Yet it was founded on a complete misinterpretation of the situation. Once she saw that, she was able to let it go and become free from the need to create abandonment every two years from that point on.

Even though she had spiritual awareness, she had consistently failed to realize that in providing instances of abandonment every two years, Spirit was in fact giving her opportunities to wake up and heal a toxic story which was a limitation on her life and a wound to her soul. Doing some forgiveness worksheets on the person who had last fired her helped her clear all the other times she had been 'abandoned' over her 52 years and neutralized her original abandonment story.

The Forgiveness Centrifuge

Using this tool might have saved both Jill, Jesse and Glenda many years of painful struggle. The Forgiveness Centrifuge helps us separate *what actually happened* in any given situation from our *interpretation* of what happened. If you own the type of juicer where you put carrots and other things in the top and the juice is separated from the fiber by the centrifugal force of the spinning grater, you know what is meant by the term centrifuge. A centrifuge also is used to separate plasma from blood, cream from milk, and so on. A washing machine spinning out the excess water from clothes works in the same manner as well.

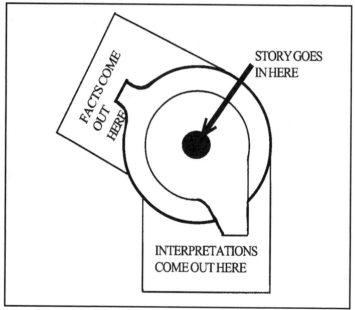

Fig. 12: Separating Fact From Fiction

A forgiveness centrifuge simply reverses the process by which we come up with stories about what happened to us. To use it, take the story you are living now — the one that is causing you discomfort. Remember, it is certain to be a hopeless mixture of fact (what happened) and interpretation (all your thoughts, judgments, assessments, assumptions, and beliefs about what happened). Feed the story into the top of the imaginary centrifuge, just like you would with carrots in a juicer, and then, in your mind, see the machine separating the facts from the interpretations.

Then, like any good researcher, first make a list of the facts as they emerge, being as objective as possible. Then make a list of the interpretations you made about the facts.

#	The Facts About What Happened

After writing down your results, acknowledge the facts and accept them. Recognize that the facts tell what happened and that no one can do anything to change that. You have no choice but to allow what happened to be exactly what happened, but watch for any tendency to make excuses for what happened. This to impose interpretation on the facts once again. Just stay with what actually happened. Next, examine every thought, belief, rationalization, idea, or attitude you imposed on what happened, and declare them all to be *untrue*. Affirm that none of them have validity. Tell yourself they just represent mind-talk.

#	My Interpretations About What Happened

Then, recognize how important your ideas, beliefs and attitudes are to you. Look at your *attachment* to each of them, and decide which of them you possibly are ready to drop and which you are not.

	Interpretations	% Attachment

Be Gentle With Yourself

Do not criticize yourself for being attached to any of them or for being unwilling to let them go. You may have had these ideas, beliefs, and attitudes for a long time. In fact, they may define who you are. For example, if you are an incest survivor or an adult child of an alcoholic, these labels, which represent ideas or beliefs about yourself, may provide a reference for who you are. If you let go of the ideas associated with these labels, you might lose your identity. So, while you want to be firm with yourself in separating what is real from what you have made up, be gentle with yourself and allow time to release these beliefs.

The next step after this is the Radical Forgiveness reframe — seeing that the story was perfect and had to play out that way. Watch out for the guilt, the anger, the depression, and the criticism you might feel and direct at yourself when you find out you have created your entire life around a set of untrue beliefs. *Please, do not do this*. Instead, remember that everything has a purpose, and God does not make mistakes. Use one or more of the forgiveness tools to work on forgiving yourself and on seeing the perfection in your situation.

If the facts still prove that something *bad* took place — for example, a murder remains a murder no matter what interpretations you may have made, the Radical Forgiveness Worksheet provides the best tool to help you shift the energy around that event.

15: RADICAL *Self*-Forgiveness

W e have learned in the foregoing chapters, I hope, that whatever we see *out there* is an outpicturing of what is *in here,* and that what we see in other people is simply a reflection of our own consciousness. If you are one of a crowd of two thousand people crammed into a room, there is, in reality, only one person in the room — and it is you. The rest of the people are reflections of you and your perception of them is simply a story that you have made up in your mind. We are always looking in the mirror, and it's all about us. In the same way therefore, *all* forgiveness is self-forgiveness.

This is what I have been arguing for a long time. Self-forgiveness happens by default as soon as your realize that what you see *out there,* is you. Once we see the truth in someone, we automatically claim it for ourselves.

It always seemed to me to be easier to forgive what was *out there,* rather than to try forgiving oneself, because we are accustomed to operating in the world as either subject or object, but never both at the same time — which is how it is with self-forgiveness. To whom are we appealing when we ask ourselves for forgiveness? Who is forgiving whom? No wonder self-forgiveness is so difficult — we are trying to be judge, jury, defendant and witness all in the same case! Better (perhaps) that we do it by radically forgiving others and, in so doing, vicariously and automatically forgiving ourselves at the same time.

This is all the more true since much of what we do hate in ourselves is unconscious, and therefore hidden from us. How can we forgive in ourselves that about which we know nothing? Fortunately, as we know, the Law of Attraction helps us out by bringing someone into our lives who will resonate those issues for us and mirror them back to us. Initially, of course, it upsets us greatly but as we do the worksheet and forgive them *(see the truth)*, we automatically forgive ourselves. That is why we say that the people we judge and dislike the most are our greatest teacher and healers.

Another reason why I resisted doing self-forgiveness work was that I had noticed that many of those who tended to want to work on forgiving themselves were often addicted to self-blame and recrimination. These people would jump at the chance to use self-forgiveness as yet another way to beat themselves up. By our insisting that they begin by first forgiving others, we not only broke their denial about not having issues with other people *(which, of course, they always did)*, but enabled them to find genuine self-forgiveness through the normal Radical Forgiveness process.

Having said all that, I recognize that there is still a need to provide the context and the spaciousness for connecting with, and extending mercy and forgiveness towards, those parts of ourselves that have assumed guilt about something that happened and/or feel shame about who we imagine ourselves to be.

For the past year, I have experimented with a self-forgiveness workshop entitled *Emergence,* and have finally proven it to be a beautiful and profoundly healing experience. Let me stress, however, that the context for this self-forgiveness work remains exactly the same as with Radical Forgiveness — that, from a spiritual viewpoint, there is no right or wrong, there are no such things as victims and perpetrators, and that there is, therefore, nothing to forgive. Consequently, the energy release obtained by virtually every participant was real and significant.

An important part of the more advanced self-forgiveness work that I am now offering has its roots in a spiritually oriented therapeutic system known as Psychosynthesis. This was founded and developed in the early 1900's by Roberto Assagioli, an Italian psychiatrist. He was way in advance of his time and is only now being fully recognized and appreciated for the work he did. I am also finding it to be quite consistent with the principles of Radical Forgiveness.

Assagioli's work showed that we have within us not just a singular inner child, as has been popularly represented, but a whole host of subpersonalities. Most of these subpersonalities were created as a way to manage or survive our primal wounds, or compensate for our perceived deficiencies — the basis of our injured sense of self.

[I should add that even people who were raised in seemingly healthy families can also be wounded. Often, wounding is subtle and can even be the result of a misperception. Spiritual wounding, too, can occur as a result of otherwise nurturing parents being themselves disconnected from Spirit or

151

presenting God as an external entity, separate from ourselves, thereby being unable to impart a spiritual connection.]

Assagioli showed that in order to get beyond these wounds and to expand into the fullness of our potential, we need to make an *empathic connection* with each of them so they can reveal themselves to us, be understood and then forgiven — in the Radical Forgiveness sense, of course. *(Caroline Myss uses a somewhat similar approach with her archetypes, as does Hal Stone with his voice dialogue technique, and David Quigley with his Alchemical Hypnotherapy).*

Earlier, it had been my intention to write another book and for it to be on the subject of self-forgiveness, but once I began writing, I realized that besides this kind of academic content, it would have been very much like this book. That's because basically, I would have been simply substituting the word perpetrator for the word victim, and that's about all the difference it would have made. Of course, there's other content that I could have added too, about dealing with and healing your own shadow, similar to that which Debbie Ford has done so well, but as far as Radical Forgiveness is concerned, it would still have been highly repetitive.

After having done several *Emergence* workshops and having become better acquainted with Assagioli's work, I realized that I needed to create, in addition to the workshops, an **online**, internet based, Radical Self-forgiveness Program that people could do in their own homes and yet achieve the same kind of results. That's what we have done.

Earlier, I raised the question regarding who is forgiving whom?

Well, there are actually two answers to that question. In the case of traditional forgiveness, the appeal is to the human self or Ego — from the Ego. Clearly, we truly are, in this instance, trying to be judge, jury, defendant and witness all in the same case. That's why it is never successful. The courtroom inside our heads remains in chaos and perpetual deadlock. I am sure many of you know what that feels like.

It is totally different with Radical Self-forgiveness. The appeal here is made, not to our human self at all, but to our Higher Self; our *I Am* consciousness. This is the transcendent part of ourself that is not separate from the All-That-Is, and, yet, is always there with us at the core of our being, observing us from above so to speak. It is also the one that knows the truth about there being no right or wrong, good or bad, and does not identify with the content or process of our life in the least. It simply observes — and its gift to me is my self-awareness.

The purpose of the Radical Self-forgiveness process, as I have come to see it, and reflect it in our workshops, in QEMS and our on-line programs, is multifaceted. In the first instance its purpose is to help us understand the nature of *self* and our relationship with those many aspects of ourselves that constitute who we are. We need first to be able to identify and then find a way to relate empathically to the various parts of ourselves that make up who we are, especially those who experienced a shortfall in their nurturing during the formative years.

Once we have identified our wounded subpersonalities and understood their need to exist as survival subpersonalities, or compensate for their perceived deficiencies, we then need to help them move beyond the wound and see the perfection in the circumstances that caused the wounding in the first place. Then we will be free to expand into who we were meant to be and come into the full realization of who we truly are. Only then will we feel unconditional love and acceptance for ourselves.

That will have brought us into full alignment with our transcendent self which knows our pure I AM perfection on the one hand and recognizes on the other, the very perfection in our imperfection.

Then we can say with full understanding of its meaning: "I'm not OK; you're not OK — but that's OK!"

NOTES:

NOTES: